99 Tricks
for
Microsoft® Project 365 and 2021

A Casual User Guide Including 2019, 2016 and 2013

By

Paul E Harris

of

Eastwood Harris Pty Ltd

99 TRICKS & TRAPS FOR MICROSOFT PROJECT 365 and 2021

©Copyright 2022 by Eastwood Harris Pty Ltd. No part of this publication may be reproduced or used in any form, electronic or print, or by any method without the written permission of the author.

Windows, XP, Windows 7, Windows 10, Windows 11 Microsoft® Project, PowerPoint, Word, Visio and Excel are registered trademarks of Microsoft Corporation.

Adobe® and Acrobat® are registered trademarks of Adobe Systems Incorporated.

All other company or product names may be trademarks of their respective owners.

Screen captures were reprinted with authorization from Microsoft Corporation.

This publication was created by Eastwood Harris Pty Ltd and is not a product of Microsoft Corporation.

DISCLAIMER

The information contained in this book is to the best of the author's knowledge true and correct. The author has made every effort to ensure accuracy of this publication but cannot be held responsible for any loss or damage arising from any information in this book.

AUTHOR AND PUBLISHER

Paul E Harris
Eastwood Harris Pty Ltd
PO Box 4032
Doncaster Heights 3109
Victoria
Australia

harrispe@eh.com.au

http://www.eh.com.au

Tel: +61 (0)4 1118 7701

Please send any comments on this publication to the author.

I would like to thank Jesica Paula Yabo for her assistance in updating this book from Microsoft Project 2007 and Martin Vaughn for proof reading and valuable suggestions.

ISBN: 978-1-925185-88-1 Paperback

ISBN: 978-1-925185-89-8 eBook

15 June 2022

99 TRICKS & TRAPS FOR MICROSOFT PROJECT 365 and 2021

CURRENT BOOKS PUBLISHED BY EASTWOOD HARRIS

Planning and Control Using Oracle Primavera P6 Versions 8 to 21 PPM Professional

99 Tricks and Traps for Oracle Primavera P6 PPM Professional - The Casual User's "Survival Guide" Updated for Version 21

Oracle Primavera P6 Version 16 EPPM Web Administrators Guide

Planning and Control Using Oracle Primavera P6 Versions 16 EPPM Web

Create and Update an Unresourced Project Using Elecosoft (Asta) Powerproject Version 16

Planning and Control Using Microsoft Project 365 and 2021 – Including 2013, 2016 and 2019

Planificación y Control Usando Oracle Primavera P6 Versiones 8.1 a 15.1 PPM Profesional

规划和控制Oracle Primavera P6 应用 版本 8.1-15.1 PPM 专业版

SERVICES OFFERED BY EASTWOOD HARRIS PTY LTD

Eastwood Harris specializes in setting up and running project controls systems with a focus on Oracle Primavera P6, Elecosoft (Asta) Powerproject and Microsoft Project software; we offer the following services:

Project Planning and Scheduling Training Courses using Oracle Primavera P6 and Microsoft Office Project

- Eastwood Harris offers one-to-one training to get your new schedulers up and running quickly, without the delay of waiting for the next course and at the same time building up your own project schedule.
- We also run in-house training courses on any of these software packages. This is a very cost-efficient method of training your personnel.
- We are able to assist you in setting up a scheduling environment. This includes designing coding structures, writing procedures, training and other implementation processes.
- Eastwood Harris can write specialized training material that will incorporate your organization's methodology into the Eastwood Harris training manuals and develop student workshops tailored to your requirements. Project personnel will be able to use these books as reference books after the course.

Selection and Implementation of Project Management Systems

- Eastwood Harris will assist you by conducting an internal review of your requirements and match this requirement analysis against the functionality of packaged software.
- We are then able to assist you in the implementation of these systems, including writing policies and procedures and training personnel, to ensure a smooth transition to your new system.

Dispute Resolution

- Eastwood Harris is able to analyze your subcontractor's schedules in the event of claims and provide you with a clear picture of the schedule in relation to the claim.

Schedule Conversion

- Eastwood Harris is able to convert your schedules from one software package to another. The conversion of schedules is often time consuming, so let us do it for you.

Please contact the author for more information on these services.

99 TRICKS & TRAPS FOR MICROSOFT PROJECT 365 and 2021

1	IMPORTANT THINGS	1
1.1	The "Delete" Key	1
1.2	Typing a Date or Dragging a Task Sets a Constraint!	1
1.3	Indicators Column	2
1.4	Why Are Tasks Scheduled before the Predecessors?	3
1.4.1	Understanding the Actual Start Date	3
1.4.2	Tasks Will Always Honor Their Constraint Dates	3
1.5	The Project Will Not Open!	5
1.6	The Logic Keeps Changing!	6
1.7	Why Do New Tasks Have an Early Start Constraint?	8
1.8	Recommended Schedule Options	9
1.9	Manually Scheduled and Auto Scheduled Tasks	10
1.10	Sorting out the Menus	11
1.11	Large Space between Mouse Buttons	13
2	CALENDAR SURVIVAL GUIDE	14
2.1	Role of the Project Calendar	14
2.2	Guidelines for Creating Calendars	15
2.3	Display of Duration in Days	16
2.4	How to Assign Task Calendars	18
2.5	Other Things Task Calendars Affect	19
2.5.1	Float	19
2.5.2	Lags	19
2.6	Resource Calendars	20
2.7	Which Calendar is the Task Using?	21
2.8	Default Start and End Time	22
2.9	Finish Variance Calculation	23
3	TRICKY STUFF	24
3.1	Task Naming Issues	24
3.2	Task Splitting	26
3.2.1	What is Splitting?	26
3.2.2	Splitting a Task Manually	27
3.2.3	Splitting In-progress Tasks	27
3.2.4	Removing a Bar Split	28
3.2.5	Hiding a Bar Split	29
3.3	Deadline Date	30
3.4	Negative and Free Float Bars	31
3.5	Where is the Gant Chart Wizard?	33
3.6	As Late As Possible Constraint	33
4	INTERESTING FEATURES	35
4.1	Wildcard Filters for Text Searching	35
4.2	Interactive Filters	36
4.3	AutoFilters	36
4.4	Selecting Dates	38
4.5	Understanding Start and Finish Milestones	38

© *Eastwood Harris*

4.6	Converting a Finish Milestone into a Start Milestone	40
4.7	Creating a Hammock or a LEO Task	41
4.8	Elapsed Durations, Leads and Lags	42
4.8.1	*Elapsed Durations*	*42*
4.8.2	*Float on Tasks with Elapsed Durations*	*42*
4.8.3	*Elapsed Leads and Lags*	*43*
4.9	Establishing Two Relationships between Two Tasks	43
4.10	Ladder scheduling	44
4.11	% Lags	45
4.12	Tracing Logic	46
4.12.1	*Task Drivers and Task Inspector*	*46*
4.12.2	*Tracing the Logic*	*48*
4.12.3	*Finding a Chain of Driving Predecessors of Successors – Displaying the Task Path*	*49*
4.12.4	*Finding Tasks with Lags*	*49*
5	**MAKING IT LOOK RIGHT**	**50**
5.1	Date Format Dangers	50
5.2	Preventing the Date Format from Changing on Other Computers	51
5.3	The Smart Way to Create Views	52
5.4	Bar Formatting	53
5.4.1	*Bar Date Format*	*53*
5.4.2	*Bar Heights*	*53*
5.4.3	*Always Roll Up Gantt Bars*	*54*
5.4.4	*Round Bars to Whole Days*	*55*
5.5	Putting Text on Bars	56
5.5.1	*Placing a Single Field on Bars*	*56*
5.6	Placing Multiple Fields in a single position on a Bar	57
5.7	Format Colors	58
5.8	How to Stop Text Wrapping	59
5.9	Text direction options	60
5.10	Display Tasks without Successors as Critical	61
5.11	Preventing Descriptions from Indenting	62
5.12	Reducing Column Widths	63
5.13	How to Display a Task ID that Will Not Change	64
5.14	Hiding Task Information	65
5.14.1	*Hiding Bars*	*65*
5.14.2	*Hiding Text*	*65*
5.14.3	*Marking Tasks Inactive*	*65*
5.15	Anchor a Vertical Line to a Milestone	66
5.16	Zoom Slider Dangers	67
5.17	Why is the Non-working Time Displayed Incorrectly?	68
5.18	Multiple Baseline Bar Display	69
5.19	Ordinal Date Display	70
5.20	Displaying an S-Curve	71

5.21	Displaying Cumulative Histogram	72
5.22	Displaying a Project Summary Task	72
6	**GETTING IT OUT - PRINTING**	**73**
6.1	Printing to One Page Wide	73
6.2	Printing a Date Range	74
6.3	Printing a Gantt Chart and Resource Graph or Usage Table on One Page	75
6.4	Printing the Calendar	75
6.5	Hiding Unwanted Bars in the Legend	76
6.6	What has Happened to the Manual Page Breaks?	76
7	**RESOURCE BASICS**	**77**
7.1	How Many Resources Should I Have?	77
7.2	The Balance Between the Number of Activities and Resources	78
7.3	Durations and Assignments Change as Resources are Assigned	79
7.3.1	*Task Type – Fixed Duration, Fixed Units, Fixed Work*	*79*
7.3.2	*Effort driven or Non Effort driven?*	*81*
7.3.3	*Task Type and Effort driven Options*	*82*
7.4	Assigning Resources to Tasks	83
7.5	Resources and Summary Tasks	83
8	**UPDATING ESSENTIALS**	**84**
8.1	Baselines and Updating a Project	84
8.2	Which Baseline Should Be Used?	85
8.3	Principles of Updating a Program	86
8.4	In-progress Task Finish Date Calculation	87
8.5	Understanding the % Completes	88
8.6	Current Date and Status Date	90
8.7	Auto Updating Using Update Project	91
8.8	Moving Incomplete Work into the Future by Splitting	92
8.9	Where is the Tracking Toolbar?	93
8.10	Why Do Calculation Options – Move end of completed parts Not Work?	95
8.11	Comparing Progress with Baseline	97
8.12	Progress Lines	97
8.13	Simple Procedure for Updating a Schedule – Using Auto Status	98
8.14	Procedure for Detailed Updating	100
8.15	Preparing to Update with Resources	102
8.16	Updating Resources	105

9	CREATING NEW PROJECTSS	106
9.1	Standardizing Projects	106
9.2	Global.mpt	106
9.3	Microsoft Project Template Changes	107
9.4	Understanding Templates	107
9.5	Eastwood Harris Template	108
9.6	Copying Views, Tables and Filters	109
10	**OTHER THINGS OF INTEREST**	**110**
10.1	Editing Tool Bars	110
10.2	Dynamically Linking Cells	111
10.3	How Does Negative Float Calculate for Summary Activities?	112
10.4	Float and Constraints	113
10.5	Using Custom Fields	114
10.6	Custom Columns Formulas and Drop-Down List	115
10.7	Creating Graphical Indicators	116
10.8	Custom Outline Codes	116
10.8.1	*Define a Custom Outline Code Structure*	*117*
10.8.2	*Assigning the Custom Codes*	*119*
10.8.3	*Grouping with Custom Data*	*120*
10.8.4	*Grouping with Custom Data with AutoFilters*	*122*
10.9	Exporting to Excel	123
10.10	Turning Off Getting Started and other POP ups	124
10.11	Contingent Time	124
10.12	Earned Value	125
10.13	Do I Have All the Scope?	126
10.13.1	*Stakeholder Analysis*	*126*
10.13.2	*Risk Analysis*	*126*
10.14	Preparing for Dispute Resolution	127
10.14.1	*Keeping Electronic Copies of Each Update*	*127*
10.14.2	*Clearly Record the Effect of Each Change*	*127*
11	**INDEX**	**129**

1 IMPORTANT THINGS

Microsoft Project 365 is a subscription version of the software and at the time of writing this book it was the same as Microsoft Project 2021.

Readers of this book should be familiar with:

- ❖ How projects are managed and the associated project management processes,
- ❖ The basic functions of Microsoft Project and
- ❖ The theory of Critical Path including Early dates, Late dates and Float calculations. Microsoft Project uses Slack for term Float.

Microsoft Project has functions that catch out users. You should understand these functions and be able to identify when they have been used inadvertently.

1.1 The "Delete" Key

Striking the delete key will delete data without warning. So keep your fingers away from it.

Note: It is recommended that you place the Tasks ID in the description of the last task so you know if you have deleted a task in error.

1.2 Typing a Date or Dragging a Task Sets a Constraint!

Functions that set a constraint without warning are:

- ❖ Typing or selecting a start date in a **Start** date field will set a **Start No Earlier Than** constraint
- ❖ Typing or selecting a finish date in a **Finish** date field will set a **Finish No Earlier Than** constraint
- ❖ Dragging a bar in the Gantt Chart View will set a **Start No Earlier Than** constraint

Note: You need to be very careful when dragging tasks or typing into date fields as this will set a constraint without warning and the tasks will not move forward in time when predecessors are removed or finished earlier.

1.3 Indicators Column

The **Indicators** column is a very useful feature that identifies when a task has an attribute that is different from a normal task which has just been created by inserting a new task. The indicators column will display a **Constraint** icon when a constraint has been set:

- Before entering a date in a Start or Finish field or Dragging a Task, the indicator column is blank:

- After entering a date in a Start or Finish field or Dragging a Task, a constraint is set. There now is a Constraint indicator in the **Indicator** column:

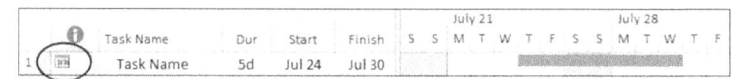

- A note is displayed when the indicator field has the mouse pointer placed over the indicator cell:

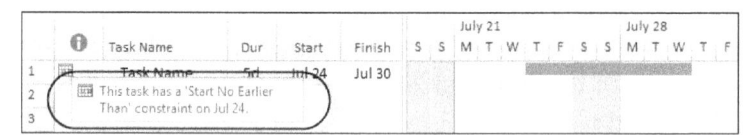

- The indicator column shows a different icon when tasks have Notes, Task Calendar or a Constraint conflict causing Negative Float (Slack):

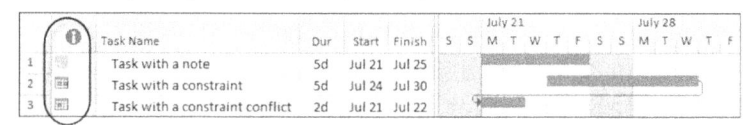

Note: No indicator is displayed with a **Deadline Date**, unless **Negative Float** is created.

1.4 Why Are Tasks Scheduled before the Predecessors?

There are a couple of reasons why tasks would be displayed before a predecessor relationship would allow them to be scheduled:

❖ An **Actual Start** date has been set, or
❖ **Tasks will always honor their constraint dates** is set and the task has a Late constraint.
  Note: This Project option should always be unchecked, see the paragraph below.

1.4.1 Understanding the Actual Start Date

An **Actual Start** is set by entering a date in the **Actual Start** field or entering a % **Complete**.

❖ Once an **Actual Start** date has been set a predecessor relationship does not affect the Actual Start date.
❖ A predecessor relationship may cause an in-progress Task with an Actual Start date to split when the **File, Options, Schedule** tab **Split in progress tasks** option has been checked.

1.4.2 Tasks Will Always Honor Their Constraint Dates

There is an option in the **File, Options, Schedule** form titled **Tasks will always honor their constraint dates**. This option forces a task to be scheduled before the predecessors when the successor has a **Finish no later than** or **Start no later than** constraint. In effect, this option will make all constraints override relationships, more on this over the page.

With this option set, a task with a **Finish No Later Than** constraint set prior to a predecessor's calculated Finish date will display an Early Finish on the constraint date and not the scheduled date. The **Total Slack** may not calculate as the difference between Late Start and Early Start.

Examine the following two examples with the option box checked and unchecked:

❖ <u>T</u>**asks will always honor their constraint dates:** option box checked:

		Start	Finish	Late Finish	Total Slack	Constraint Date	Constraint Type
1		Jul 21	Jul 25	Jul 23	-2d	NA	As Soon As Possible
2		Jul 28	Jul 29	Jul 25	-2d	NA	As Soon As Possible
3		Jul 25	Jul 25	Jul 25	-2d	Jul 25	Finish No Later Than

Task 3 starts before the predecessor finishes and the Total Slack of the second task is calculated as minus 2 days, which is not the difference between the Early Finish and the Late Finish dates. This constraint does not adhere to commonly accepted Total Float calculations.

❖ <u>T</u>**asks will always honor their constraint dates**: option box NOT checked and the Total Float is calculated correctly:

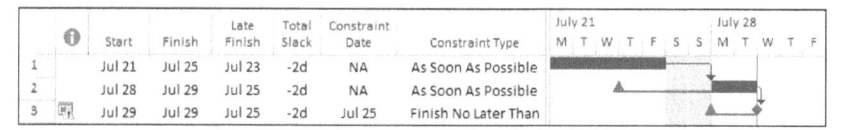

		Start	Finish	Late Finish	Total Slack	Constraint Date	Constraint Type
1		Jul 21	Jul 25	Jul 23	-2d	NA	As Soon As Possible
2		Jul 28	Jul 29	Jul 25	-2d	NA	As Soon As Possible
3		Jul 29	Jul 29	Jul 25	-2d	Jul 25	Finish No Later Than

Note: It is suggested that this option is **<u>NEVER</u>** switched on, as the schedule may appear to be achievable when it is not.

1.5 The Project Will Not Open!

All Microsoft Project files have a ***.mpp** file extension, so it is difficult to determine the version that a Microsoft Project file was created with.

- Microsoft Project 365, 2021, 2019, 2016, 2013 and 2010 share the same format and may not be opened by earlier versions of Microsoft Project.
- Microsoft Project 365, 2021, 2019, 2016, 2013 and 2010 may save to 2007 and
- 2016, 2013 and 2010 may also save to 2000-2003 format.

The **File**, **Options**, **Trust Center**, **Trust Center Settings…**, **Legacy Format** option also determines if you are able to open earlier formats, it is recommended that you select the **Prompt when loading files with legacy or non-default file format** so you will know when you are opening an earlier file format.

When saving to earlier versions there may be a loss of data and different software versions can result in different calculations in some circumstances. For example, Microsoft Project 2000-2003 format does not support either **Cost Resources** or the naming of **Calendar Nonworking Days**.

You should use the **Gantt Chart Wizard** to format the bars when opening a project from Microsoft Project 2016, 2013 or 2010 that was created with Microsoft Project 2007 or earlier version. If you use the Ribbon functionalities, the baseline will be hidden behind the current bars.

Note: One of the well know methods of obtaining a corrupt file is to work in older versions or changing version formats on a regular basis and both these practices should be avoided.

1.6 The Logic Keeps Changing!

The logic will change if a task is dragged to another position when **File, Options, Schedule** tab, **Autolink inserted or moved tasks** option checked.

This option is intended to be used to automatically link new inserted tasks with a predecessor to the task above and a successor to the task below.

The downside of this function is that when the task is moved this function will change the existing predecessors and successors of the following:

- Moved task,
- Original tasks that were above and below the moved task, and
- New tasks that are now above and below the moved tasks.

This function will potentially make substantial changes to your project logic and may affect the overall project duration.

Note: It is strongly recommended that this option is **NEVER** switched on, as dragging an activity to a new location may completely change the logic of a schedule without warning.

An example of this process is shown below:

❖ Original Logic:

	Task Name	Dur	Predecessors	Successors	July 21 M T W T F S S	July 28 M T W T F
1	A	2d		2		
2	B	2d	1	3		
3	C	2d	2	4		
4	D	2d	3	5		
5	E	2d	4			

❖ Task D dragged with **<u>A</u>utolink inserted or moved tasks** checked. Note the logic has changed on many tasks:

	Task Name	Dur	Predecessors	Successors	July 21 M T W T F S S	July 28 M T W T F
1	A	2d		3,2		
2	D	2d	4,1	5		
3	B	2d	1	4		
4	C	2d	3	2,5		
5	E	2d	2,4			

❖ Task D dragged with **<u>A</u>utolink inserted or moved tasks** unchecked. The logic has not changed:

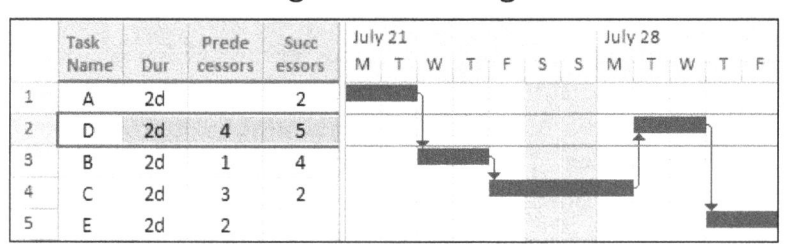

	Task Name	Dur	Predecessors	Successors	July 21 M T W T F S S	July 28 M T W T F
1	A	2d		2		
2	D	2d	4	5		
3	B	2d	1	4		
4	C	2d	3	2		
5	E	2d	2			

1.7 Why Do New Tasks Have an Early Start Constraint?

Unlike other scheduling software, Microsoft Project normally ignores the **Status Date** when calculating a schedule with progress. It schedules tasks without an Actual Start or predecessors or constraints on the **Project Start Date**, or as close to the **Project Start Date** as calendars permit. It does not automatically schedule the incomplete portions of Tasks after the **Status Date**.

The **File, Options, Schedule** tab has an **Auto scheduled tasks scheduled on:** option that may be set to either:

- **Start on Current Date**, or
- **Start on Project Start Date**.

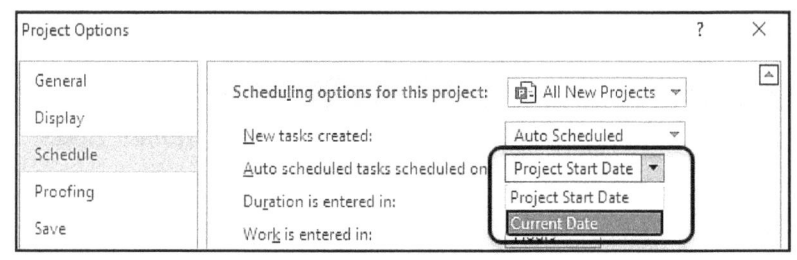

- When set to start on **Current Date**, new tasks are created with an **Early Start Constraint** set to the **Current Date**, which is set to the current date of the computers operating system, e.g. today's date.
- When set to start on **Project Start Date**, new tasks are created without a constraint and all new tasks will schedule on the **Project Start Date**. This is the recommended setting and new tasks will not be assigned a constraint when created.

1.8 Recommended Schedule Options

It is best to keep a schedule as simple as possible. It is recommended that you consider the following **File, Schedule, Options** as a good starting point if you have limited experience in scheduling software.

If you ensure **ALL PROJECTS ARE CLOSED** before you start setting your options then all changes that you make to the options will be applied to new projects created using the **File, New** command which uses your **Global.mpt** template:

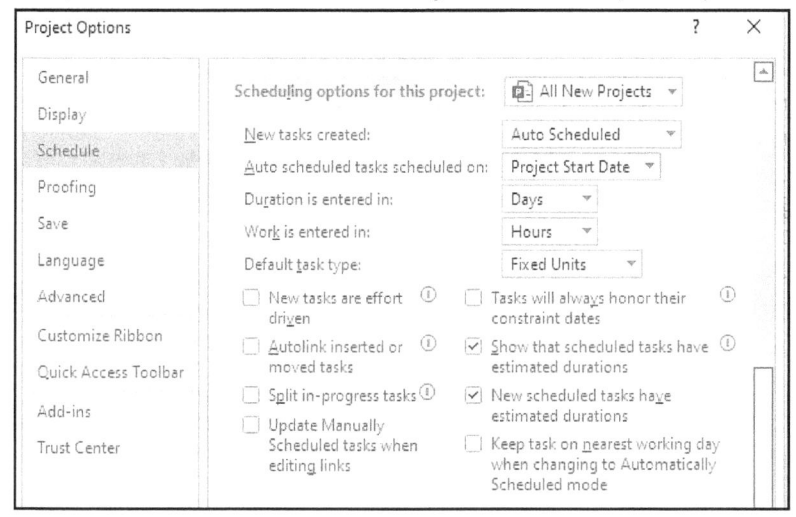

Project Options		
General	Scheduling options for this project:	All New Projects
Display	New tasks created:	Auto Scheduled
Schedule	Auto scheduled tasks scheduled on:	Project Start Date
Proofing	Duration is entered in:	Days
Save	Work is entered in:	Hours
Language	Default task type:	Fixed Units
Advanced	☐ New tasks are effort driven	☐ Tasks will always honor their constraint dates
Customize Ribbon	☐ Autolink inserted or moved tasks	☑ Show that scheduled tasks have estimated durations
Quick Access Toolbar	☐ Split in-progress tasks	☑ New scheduled tasks have estimated durations
Add-ins	☐ Update Manually Scheduled tasks when editing links	☐ Keep task on nearest working day when changing to Automatically Scheduled mode
Trust Center		

Note: Most of the other options are covered in this book but the options that must be switched off to ensure the software operates in a predictable way are:

- ❖ **Autolink inserted or moved tasks**,
- ❖ **Split in-progress tasks**, and
- ❖ **Tasks will always honor their constraint dates**.

1.9 Manually Scheduled and Auto Scheduled Tasks

The **File, Options, Schedule, New tasks created:** allows the selection of **Manually Scheduled** or **Auto Scheduled**.

- ❖ The **Manually Scheduled** option (new to Microsoft Project 2010) overrides the schedule calculations for tasks marked as **Manually Scheduled**, allowing the software to be used like a white board for the selected tasks.
- ❖ It is normally considered good scheduling to select **Auto Scheduled** so tasks will acknowledge the relationships and constraints.
- ❖ Therefore, the **File, Options, Schedule, New tasks created:** should always be set to **Auto Scheduled**.

If your schedule is behaving strangely or there is unfamiliar bar formatting, this could be because some tasks have become **Manually Scheduled**. To fix this you may either:

- ❖ Display the **Task Mode** column and search for Manually Scheduled tasks and fix them in the column, or
- ❖ Click on the **Select All** button and then click on the **Auto Schedule** button.

Note: Sometimes Microsoft Project will change a Task from **Manually Scheduled** to **Auto Scheduled** without a warning and then the schedule will start behaving strangely. So, when a schedule does not reschedule correctly or there are some strange looking bars you should apply the **Manually Scheduled** filter and change any **Manually Scheduled** tasks to **Auto Scheduled**. The Eastwood Harris Microsoft Project Template has been edited to ensure all Manually scheduled tasks are displayed with a turquoise bar over the top of all other bars. This may be downloaded from **www.eh.com.au**, **Software and Downloads** page.

1.10 Sorting out the Menus

The grouping of the Ribbon commands is by software functions; such as Project, Task etc. and not by scheduling functions such as creating or updating. Therefore, users continually swap from one Ribbon menu to another while operating the software. There are some actions you should consider changing on your menus to make the software easier to use:

❖ Right click on the Ribbon toolbar to open a menu:

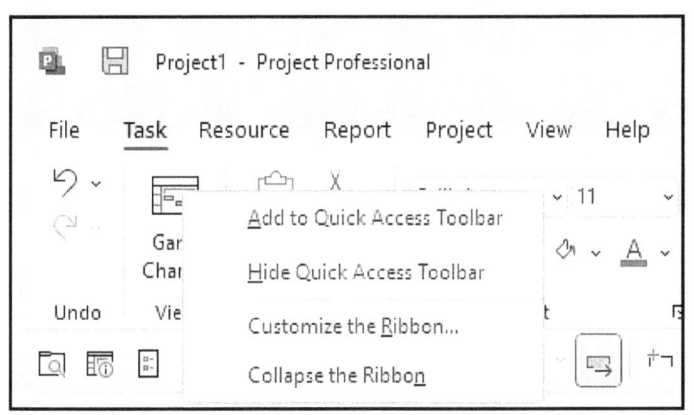

❖ The **Quick Access Toolbar** should be moved below the Ribbon Toolbar by clicking on the **Show Quick Access Toolbar Below the Ribbon**. This option allows more buttons to be displayed and the toolbar is not truncated by the **Project Name** at the top of the screen.

❖ The **Collapse the Ribbon...** command hides the Ribbon Toolbar and just leaves the menu displayed at the top, providing more screen space. This was called **Minimize the Ribbon** in Microsoft Project 2010. Clicking on one of the menu commands will display the Ribbon Toolbar.

❖ You should build your own Quick Access Toolbar by using the **Customize Quick Access Toolbar...** option which opens the **Project Options** form **Quick Access Toolbar** tab where buttons may be added to or removed from or reordered on the Quick Access Toolbar.

❖ The **Add to Quick Access Toolbar** command will add a selected Ribbon Toolbar button to the Quick Access Toolbar. By default, the Quick Access Toolbar is positioned at the top left-hand side of the screen and is always displayed.

Note: To do all these changes in one hit, you should consider downloading the Eastwood Harris Quick Access toolbar from **www.eh.com.au**, **Software & Downloads** page and import it from the **File**, **Options**, **Quick Access toolbar**, **Import/Export** command.

Microsoft Project 2021 changed the **Format** menu to be prefixed with the data type that is being formatted, see the picture below where **Format** has been changed to **Gantt Chart Format**:

Microsoft Project 2021

Microsoft Project 2016 and 2019

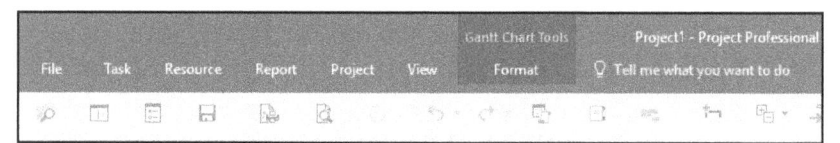

Microsoft Project 2016

Microsoft Project 2013

1.11 Large Space between Mouse Buttons

The **Touch/Mouse Mode** makes the space between the icons on all the Toolbars wider for people using a touch mouse, but you will see fewer commands.

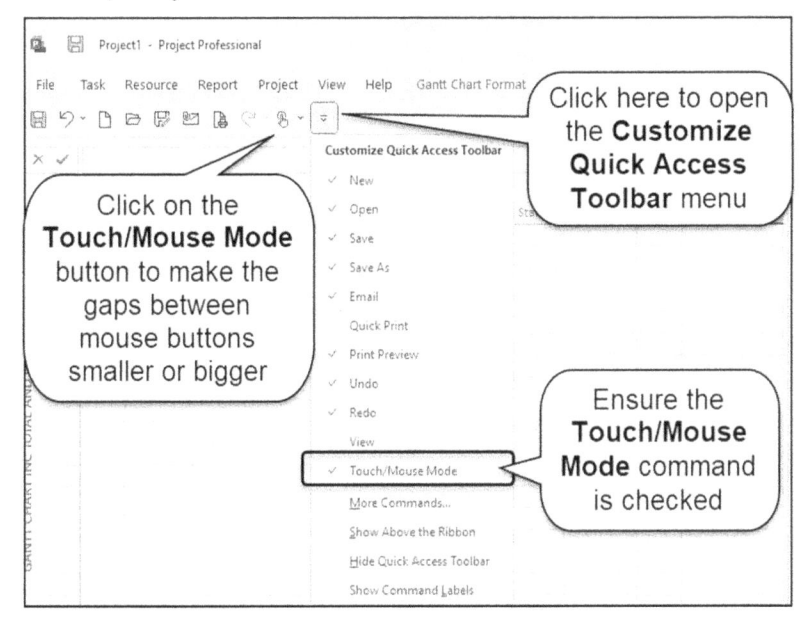

[Screenshot showing the Customize Quick Access Toolbar menu with annotations:
- "Click here to open the **Customize Quick Access Toolbar** menu"
- "Click on the **Touch/Mouse Mode** button to make the gaps between mouse buttons smaller or bigger"
- "Ensure the **Touch/Mouse Mode** command is checked"]

To increase or decrease the spacing between the mouse buttons you should:

❖ Add the **Touch/Mouse Mode** button to the **Quick Access** toolbar by clicking on the last button on the **Quick Access** toolbar titled **Customize Quick Access Toolbar**,

❖ This will open a menu and make sure **Touch/Mouse Mode** is checked as per the picture above to add it to the **Quick Access** toolbar,

❖ Then click on the button to add or remove the large spaces on the toolbar.

2 CALENDAR SURVIVAL GUIDE

2.1 Role of the Project Calendar

The project calendar is assigned to a project in the **File**, **Info**, **Project Information** form:

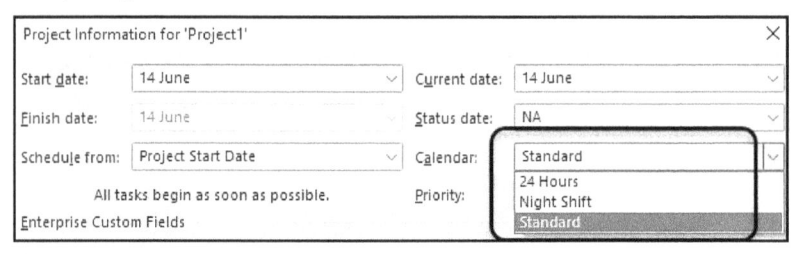

Project Information for 'Project1'				✕
Start date:	14 June	Current date:	14 June	
Finish date:	14 June	Status date:	NA	
Schedule from:	Project Start Date	Calendar:	Standard	
	All tasks begin as soon as possible.	Priority:	24 Hours / Night Shift / **Standard**	
Enterprise Custom Fields				

❖ New tasks are not assigned a calendar by default.

❖ All tasks that have not been assigned a Task Calendar calculate their Early Finish date from their Early Start date plus the Duration calculated from the Project Calendar.

❖ Therefore, a five-day duration task with a five-day workweek calendar, starting Wednesday, with Saturday and Sunday as non workdays, will finish at the end of the workday on the following Tuesday, see the picture below:

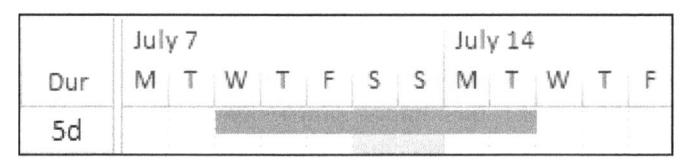

Dur	July 7							July 14				
	M	T	W	T	F	S	S	M	T	W	T	F
5d												

Note: A change to the **Project Calendar** may make substantial changes to the elapsed duration of all activities that have not been assigned a Task Calendar.

2.2 Guidelines for Creating Calendars

Calendars are created and edited using the **Project**, **Project**, **Change Working Time** form.

An unlimited number of calendars may be created:

- One calendar is assigned as the Project Calendar.
- Each task and resource may be assigned a unique calendar.
- The calendar assigned to a resource may be further edited to represent the resource's unique availability.

There are some guidelines that should be considered when contemplating the use of multiple calendars. These are summarized below:

- If you are able to schedule a project with only one calendar, then do so, thus keeping the schedule simple.
- The work hours per day for all calendars on a project should be the same for each workday, otherwise the Summary Task Durations in days will not all calculate correctly.
- Keep the Start and Finish times for all calendars the same, otherwise the Default Start and Finish Time will be incorrect for some tasks when Constraints or Actual Dates are assigned without times being displayed.
- When resources are assigned to a task without a **Task Calendar** then the **Resource Calendar** takes preference over the **Project Calendar**, unless **Scheduling ignores resource calendars** is checked in the **Task Information** form.

2.3   Display of Duration in Days

Microsoft Project effectively calculates in hours. The value of the duration in days is calculated using the parameter entered in the **Hours per day:** field in the **File, Options, Schedule, Calendar options for this project** section. It is **VERY IMPORTANT** to understand that all durations in days are calculated using **ONLY** this parameter with **EVERY** calendar irrespective of the number of hours per day in any calendar.

For example, when the **Options** form **Hours per day:** value is set to "8" then tasks assigned:

❖ An 8-hours per day calendar will have durations in days displayed correctly, and

❖ A 24-hours per day calendar will have durations in days displayed incorrectly,

The picture below shows:

❖ Task 1 has the correct duration of 5 days, but

❖ Task 2 also shows a 5-day duration that is clearly misleading.

	Task Calendar	Dur	S	S	M	T	W	T	F	S	S
1	8 Hours per Day	5d									
2	24 Hours per Day	5d									

❖ Tasks 4 and 5 display the duration in hours and this is not as misleading because the calendar column is also displayed.

	Task Calendar	Dur	S	S	M	T	W	T	F	S	S
4	8 Hours per Day	40h									
5	24 Hours per Day	40h									

It is **STRONGLY RECOMMENDED** that you avoid assigning calendars with a different number of hours per day wherever possible.

There are some workable options to ensure that the durations in days are calculated and/or displayed correctly:

- ❖ All the calendars used on a project schedule should have the same number of hours per day for each day. This value is entered in the **Hours per day:** field in the **File**, **Options**, **Schedule** tab.

- ❖ When there is a requirement to use a different number of hours per day (in either the same calendar or in different calendars) then all durations should only be displayed in hours and the Task Calendar should also displayed in a column. The **Duration is entered in:** field in the **File, Options, Schedule, Scheduling options for this project** section should be set to **Hours**. Thus, all durations will be entered by default in hours.

- ❖ A **Customized Field** may be used to calculate and display the correct duration in days using a formula. The formula below may be used to calculate the correct duration in a **Duration** Customized Field of tasks scheduled on a 24 hours per day calendar when the Project Calendar is an 8 hour per day calendar:

    IIf([Task Calendar]="24 hr/day",[Duration]*0.33,[Duration])

2.4 How to Assign Task Calendars

A task may be assigned a calendar that is different from the Project Calendar by:

- Displaying the **Task Calendar** column and editing the Task Calendar from this column, or
- Double-clicking on the task to open the **Task Information** form and selecting the **Advanced** tab.

After a calendar has been assigned, an icon will appear in the **Indicators** column and the calendar name displayed in the Task Calendar column, as shown in the picture below for the **Installation Requirements** task:

		Task Name	Task Calendar
1		Technical Feasibility Study	None
2	📅	Installation Requirements	6 Day Working Week
3		Component Bids	None

- The task Finish date, Total Float, Free Float and Variances from a Baseline will be calculated on the Task Calendar. This often leads to confusion for new users as tasks on a 24-hour/day calendar will have different Float than tasks on an 8-hour/day calendar.
- When resources are assigned to a Task, the Finish date is calculated on the Resource calendar; unless the Task has been assigned a calendar and the box in the **Task Information** form **Advanced** tab **Scheduling ignores resource calendars** is checked, then the task duration is calculated based on the assigned Task Calendar.

2.5 Other Things Task Calendars Affect

Microsoft Project use the term **Slack** whereas most textbooks and contracts sue the term **Float**. They are used interchangeably.

2.5.1 Float

Float (Slack) is calculated on the Task Calendar. Both tasks below have been scheduled to finish at 17:00 hours but have different Float values:

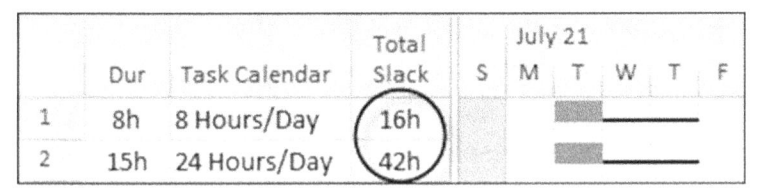

	Dur	Task Calendar	Total Slack	July 21 S M T W T F
1	8h	8 Hours/Day	16h	
2	15h	24 Hours/Day	42h	

2.5.2 Lags

Lags are calculated on the **Successor Calendar**, and therefore affect the start date and time of successors:

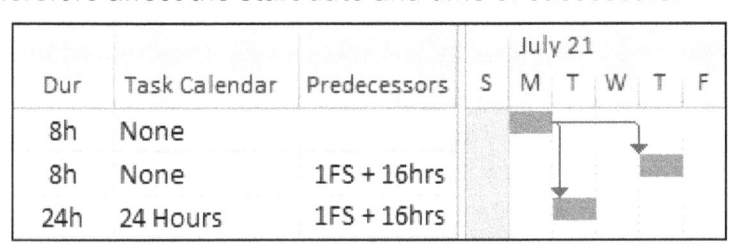

Dur	Task Calendar	Predecessors	July 21 S M T W T F
8h	None		
8h	None	1FS + 16hrs	
24h	24 Hours	1FS + 16hrs	

Note: Microsoft Project 2000 uses the **Project Calendar** to calculate lags, therefore files may calculate differently in 2000 from later versions. The example below is the file from the picture above and opened in Microsoft Project 2000:

Duration	Task Calendar	Predecessors	2 April S M T W T F
8 hrs	None		
8 hrs	None	1FS+16 hrs	
24 hrs	24 Hours	1FS+16 hrs	

2.6 Resource Calendars

Each resource is created with its very own editable calendar. Here are some important points:

- ❖ Each new resource is assigned a copy of the current **Project Calendar** as its **Base Calendar**.
- ❖ This Resource Base Calendar may be changed in the **Resource Sheet** or **Change Working Time** form to another Base Calendar.
- ❖ Any change to a Base Calendar will be reflected in any Resource Calendar.
- ❖ The Resource Calendar may be edited to suit the availability of the resource. Days may be made non workdays to represent holidays, etc.
- ❖ Normally the duration of a resourced task is calculated from the Resource Calendar.
- ❖ A task will finish at the end of the longest resource assignment when there are two or more resources assigned to a task that have different end dates due to different Resource calendars or assignment durations.
- ❖ When a Task has been assigned a calendar and the check box in the **Task Information** form, **Advanced** tab, **Scheduling ignores resource calendars** is checked, then the task duration is then calculated from the Task calendar.
- ❖ The Finish date may be calculated differently after a task is assigned one or more resources when the Resources Calendars are not the same as the Task Calendar.

2.7 Which Calendar Is the Task Using?

Try the checklist below when it is difficult to understand which calendar is being used for calculating a task Finish date:

- Check the Project Calendar in the **Project, Project, Project Information...** form,
- Then check the Task Calendar in the **Task Information** form **Advanced** tab or a Task Calendar column,
- Next check if resources are assigned to the task,
- Finally check the Resource Calendar for holidays.

The rules are as follows:

- When NO Task Calendar and NO resources are assigned, then the Project Calendar is used.
- When a Task Calendar is assigned and there are NO resources assigned then the Task Calendar is being used.
- When Resources are assigned and NO Task Calendar then the Resource Calendar is used.
- When Resources and a Task Calendar are assigned, then the commonly available time from both calendars is used to schedule the task.
- When Resources and a Task Calendar are assigned and the **Scheduling ignores resource calendars** is checked, the Task Calendar is used.

Note: A common mistake is assigning a task an edited task calendar, then at a later date assigning resources without editing the resource calendars to match the task calendars and not realizing that the task durations no longer calculate the same.

2.8　Default Start and End Time

You may notice tasks span one day longer in the bar chart than their duration. This often occurs when the calendar start and finish times are edited but the **Default start time:** and **Default end time:** set in the **File, Options, Schedule** form, **Calendar options for this project** are not adjusted to match the task calendars.

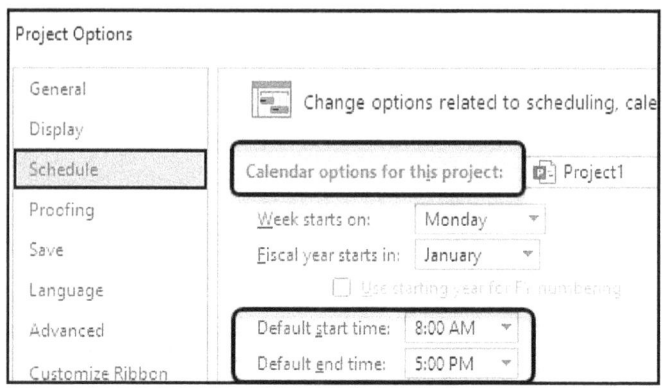

The software assigns a **Default start time:** and **Default end time:** when a date is entered in a field, but a time is not entered. This will happen when your date format does not include the time.

These times **MUST** be aligned to the Project Calendar when:

❖ Constraints are assigned to tasks, and

❖ Actual Start or Actual Finish dates are assigned.

When these times are not aligned then tasks may be displayed one day longer than their assigned duration. The picture below shows a 3-day task spanning four days because the Calendar start time is 8:00 am and the Default start time is 9:00 am.

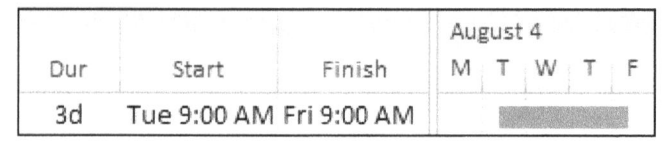

These times are set in the **Project Options** form, **Schedule** tab which may be accessed by:

- Clicking the [Options...] button in the **Project**, **Properties** tab, **Change Working Time** form, or
- Selecting the **File, Options, Schedule** tab. To assist in reading and interpretation of a schedule that has calendars with different start or finish times then:
- The Task Calendar should be displayed in columns, and
- The time should be displayed with the date in start and finish columns by selecting **File, Options, General** tab, **Project View** section and selecting an appropriate date format.

2.9 Finish Variance Calculation

The **Finish Variance** is only calculated on **Baseline** date and **Duration** fields, and not **Baseline 1** to **Baseline 10**.

- The **Finish Variance** is the difference between the **Early Finish** and **Baseline Finish**.
- Variances are calculated on the Task Calendar.

The picture below shows two milestones that have their Baselines set and have been delayed one week:

Task Calendar	Finish Variance	August 4 M T W T F S S	August 11 M T W
5 Days per Week	5 days	◇	◆
7 Days per Week	7 days	◇	◆

- The milestone on a 5-day per week calendar has a 5-day variance which is not the elapsed variance, and
- The milestone on a 7-day per week calendar has a 7-day variance which is the elapsed variance.

Note: When you need to calculate a milestone variance in calendar days, it is best to place the milestone on a 7-day per week calendar without holidays to ensure the Variance calculates the elapsed duration.

3 TRICKY STUFF

3.1 Task Naming Issues

It is often best in Microsoft Project to make all Task Names unique, so for example when you have a building with many floors and trades (skills or crafts) each Task Name should include the trade and floor.

❖ This makes it easier to understand the schedule when a filter has been applied and to find predecessors and successors in a large schedule.

❖ In Microsoft Project 2010, 2013 and earlier versions of 2016 this is even more important because the tasks are listed in the predecessor and successor lists in alphabetical order and not the order in the schedule. So if you have 20 Floors with a concrete activity titled "Concrete", then these activities will be listed all together in a list and it will be difficult to know which floor each concrete task belongs too.

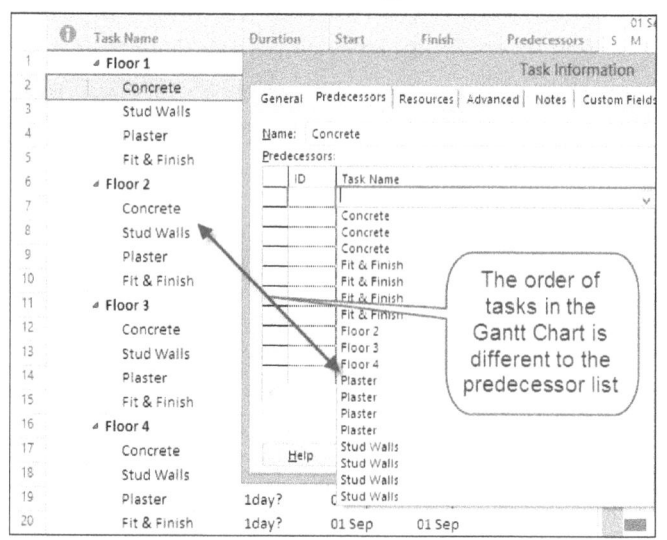

The order of tasks in the Gantt Chart is different to the predecessor list

Note: This issue was resolved with automatic updates in Microsoft Project 2016 in late 2017.

These descriptions may be created in a spreadsheet by using the **Concatenate** function, the picture below demonstrates how. Text may be added by including it in double quotation marks:

	A	B	C
1	Floor 1	Concrete Works	=A1&" - "&B1
2	Floor 1	Frame Walls	Floor 1 - Frame Walls
3	Floor 1	Hang Wall Sheeting	Floor 1 - Hang Wall Sheeting
4	Floor 2	Concrete Works	Floor 2 - Concrete Works
5	Floor 2	Frame Walls	Floor 2 - Frame Walls
6	Floor 2	Hang Wall Sheeting	Floor 2 - Hang Wall Sheeting
7	Floor 3	Concrete Works	Floor 3 - Concrete Works
8	Floor 3	Frame Walls	Floor 3 - Frame Walls
9	Floor 3	Hang Wall Sheeting	Floor 3 - Hang Wall Sheeting

As you can see below the tasks are now listed in "Floor" order in the predecessor list.

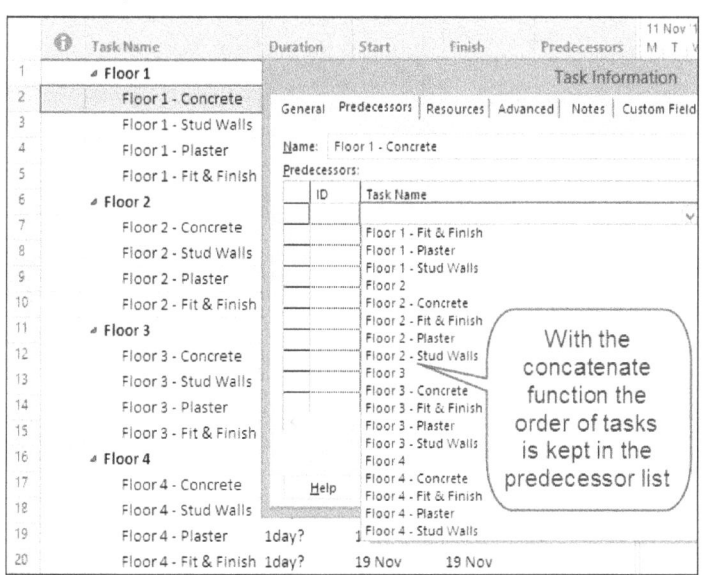

With the concatenate function the order of tasks is kept in the predecessor list

Note: When inserting the **Task Name** column you will find it is titled **Name**.

3.2 Task Splitting

3.2.1 What is Splitting?

Splitting a task puts one or more breaks in a Task, leaving:

❖ The Duration value unchanged with a **Fixed Units** task but the elapsed duration is increased,

❖ The Duration value changed with a **Fixed Duration** task to equal the elapsed duration, and

❖ Resources assigned to a split task are not assigned work during the splits:

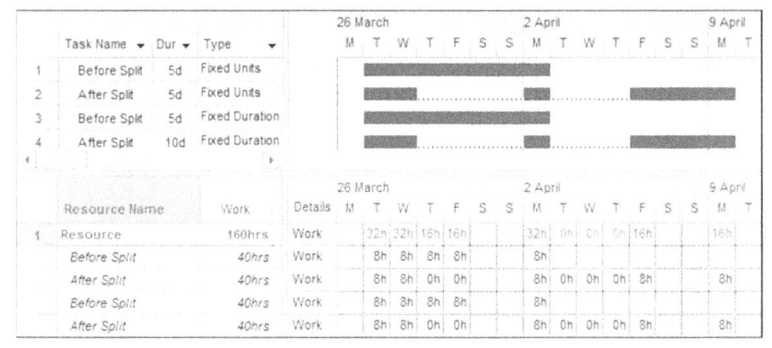

In the picture ablove you will see that Work is not scheduled during the split.

3.2.2 Splitting a Task Manually

To split a task manually,

- ❖ Left-click on the [icon] **Split Task** button located on the **Task** toolbar, **Schedule** section,
- ❖ The **Split Task:** box will appear,
- ❖ Click on the point on the Gantt Chart bar where the split is to be made and click.
- ❖ Then drag the task:

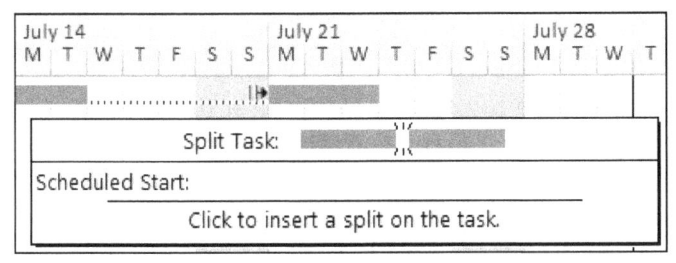

Note:

The finish and start dates and times of each split are not available through the user interface.

3.2.3 Splitting In-progress Tasks

When the **Split in-progress tasks** option is enabled in the **File, Options, Schedule** form, a task will **Split** automatically when a task commences before its predecessor finishes.

Note: This function is similar to the Primavera **Retained Logic** function and often produces unwanted Negative Slack.

3.2.4 Removing a Bar Split

A split is removed by:

- ❖ A manually created split is removed by dragging the split part back with the mouse.
- ❖ An automatically created split is removed by Turning off **Split in-progress tasks** in the **File**, **Options**, **Schedule** form.

Notes:

- ❖ You therefore need to pay careful attention to any warning messages Microsoft Project presents, if you have not switched the warning messages off.
- ❖ Sometimes a tail of dots is left after the split has been removed from a **Fixed Duration** task. This is the result of a split at the end of a task. This tail has to be dragged back to the finish of the task using the mouse and then the **Duration** reset for the task to calculate correctly:

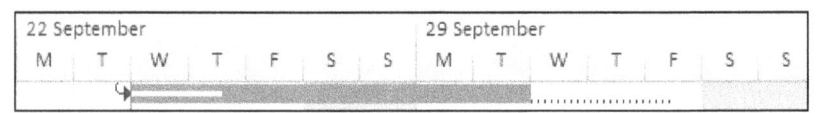

Also, you may receive a split at the start of a task when the **File**, **Options**, **Schedule**, **Split in-progress** option is selected and an Actual Start Date is set earlier than the predecessor finish. To prevent this either:

- ❖ Turn off Automatic scheduling before updating the task, then press F9 to recalculate the schedule or
- ❖ Set the Actual Duration before entering the Actual Start.

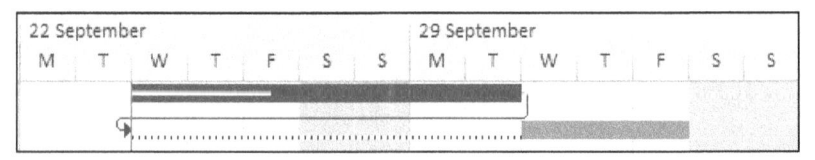

3.2.5 Hiding a Bar Split

Even though the task has been split, bar splits may be hidden by:

❖ Selecting **Gantt Chart Format**, **Format**, **Layout** to open the **Layout** form and

❖ Uncheck the **Show bar splits**.

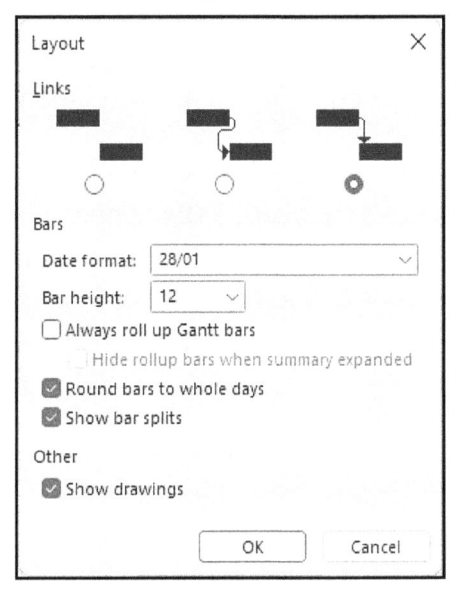

❖ The 10-day **Fixed Units** activity below has a split with an elapsed duration of 17 days:

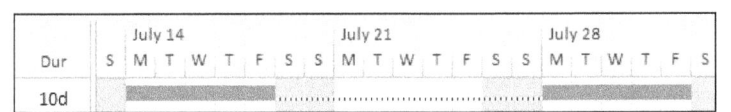

❖ The 10-day activity below has a hidden split and an elapsed duration of 17 days, which may be misleading:

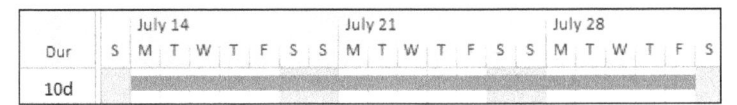

29 © Eastwood Harris

3.3 Deadline Date

Microsoft Project does not allow setting two task constraints; except in the case of a **Deadline Date**.

- A **Deadline Date** is set in the **Task Information** form **Advanced** tab or in the **Deadline Date** column.
- **Deadline Date** allows the setting of a date by which a task should be completed.
- A **Deadline Date** is similar to placing a **Finish No Later Than** constraint and affects the calculation of the **Late Finish** date and float of the activity.
- A constraint such as an Early Start constraint may also be assigned to a task with a Deadline Date.
- The Deadline Date may be displayed as a column and appears on the bar chart as a down arrow ⇩.
- An Indicator icon is placed in the **Indicator** column when the Deadline Date creates Negative Float (Slack).
- The picture below shows how a Deadline Date is displayed, this allows the date to be changed by dragging the ⇩ icon in the Gantt chart.
- It also displays how Negative Float is calculated when the Deadline Date is set before the Task Early Finish.

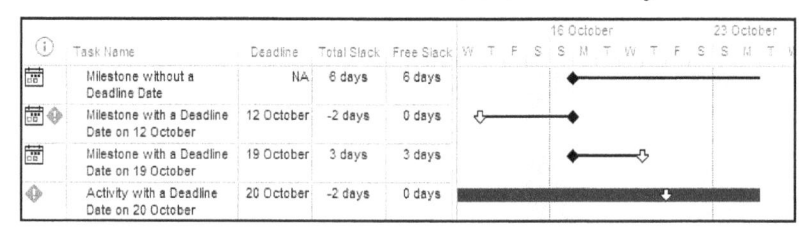

Task Name	Deadline	Total Slack	Free Slack
Milestone without a Deadline Date	NA	6 days	6 days
Milestone with a Deadline Date on 12 October	12 October	-2 days	0 days
Milestone with a Deadline Date on 19 October	19 October	3 days	3 days
Activity with a Deadline Date on 20 October	20 October	-2 days	0 days

3.4 Negative and Free Float Bars

There are some issues with the default Microsoft Project 365, 2021, 2019, 2016 and 2013 bar formatting:

❖ By default, Microsoft project only displays the **Free Float Bar** with the **Gantt Chart Format**, **Bar Styles** group, **Slack** button not the **Total Float Bar** that would normally be expected.

❖ Also, the **Negative Float Bar** is not automatically displayed by any Microsoft Project function, nor is it included in any standard View.

These are two of the most important bars to show when a project finish date has been set using a constraint and these bars must always be manually created.

❖ **Negative Float** is generated when the Late date is calculated earlier than the Early date and represents the amount of time that the schedule must catch up or how much earlier a project must start to finish on time. Setting a Late constraint or Deadline date earlier than the calculated Early Finish date normally causes Negative Float.

❖ **Free Float** is the amount of time a task may be delayed without delaying a successor task.

These two float bars will have to be added manually using the **Bar Style** form by:

❖ Selecting **Gantt Chart Format**, **Bar Styles**, **Format** drop down box, **Bar Styles** or double-click anywhere in the Gantt Chart area except on an existing bar (this will open the **Format Bar** form and not the **Bar Styles** form) to format an individual bar.

❖ Then add the additional bars as indicated below:

Name	Appearance	Show For ... Tasks	Row	From	To
Total Foat			1	Task Finish	Total Slack
Neg Float			1	Negative Slack	Task Start

Note: Unlike some other software, the **Negative Float** is drawn from the Start Date of a task and not the Finish Date. Therefore, one bar is required for Negative Float and one for Positive Float.

There are some options to permanently resolve this lack of formatting functionality:

❖ You may wish to consider recording a macro to create the bars and this can be run when a Total Float and Negative Float bar is required.

❖ You could create a **View** with these bars, save your own template with this view and then use the template to create all new projects.

❖ The author has found that these additional bars produce a better presentation and do not interfere with the drawing of relationships when created at the bottom of the list in the Bar Styles form.

❖ You may also download an Eastwood Harris Microsoft Project 365, 2021, 2019, 2016 and 2013 template project from the Eastwood Harris web site at **www.eh.com.au**, **Software & Downloads** page. This has an inbuilt View which displays both the Total and Negative Float bars. Also, other issues with Microsoft Project 365, 2021, 2019, 2016 and 2013 have been resolved and are covered in the template description on the web site.

3.5 Where Is the Gant Chart Wizard?

The **Gantt Chart Wizard** was the main method of formatting the bars in Microsoft Project 2007 and earlier.

It is still available in Microsoft Project 2019, 2016, 2013 and 2010 and may be accessed by adding ⬛ icon to the Ribbon or Quick Access toolbar.

The **Gantt Chart Wizard** should only be used to format projects created with Microsoft Project 2007 and earlier. If it is used to format projects created with Microsoft Project 2019 or 2016 or 2013 or 2010 then some strange things happen like the Baseline bars cover up the current schedule Summary bars.

3.6 As Late As Possible Constraint

This constraint must be used with caution as it consumes Total Float (Slack) and therefore delays all successor activities; it does not just delay the task that the constraint is applied to.

❖ All Tasks in the picture below have Total Float:

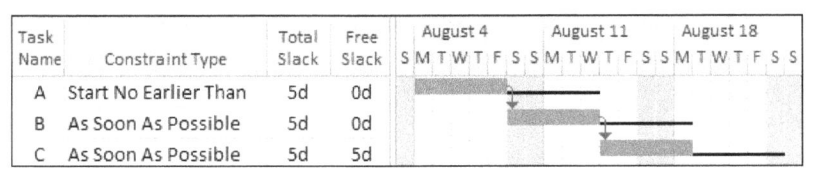

Task Name	Constraint Type	Total Slack	Free Slack
A	Start No Earlier Than	5d	0d
B	As Soon As Possible	5d	0d
C	As Soon As Possible	5d	5d

❖ When Task C is made As Late As Possible then Task B develops Free Float:

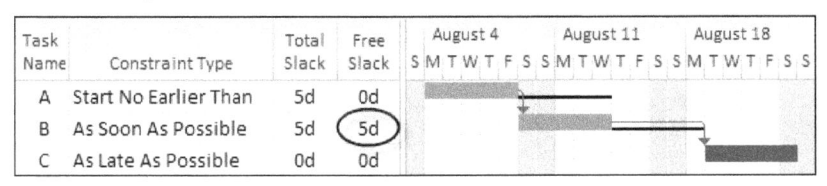

Task Name	Constraint Type	Total Slack	Free Slack
A	Start No Earlier Than	5d	0d
B	As Soon As Possible	5d	5d
C	As Late As Possible	0d	0d

❖ When Task C is made **As Soon As Possible** and Task A is made **As Late As Possible** then Task A consumes all available Total Float and delays all the successors:

Task Name	Constraint Type	Total Slack	Free Slack
A	As Late As Possible	0d	0d
B	As Soon As Possible	0d	0d
C	As Soon As Possible	0d	0d

Note: Some software packages offer a **Zero Total Float** function, which allows activities to be delayed and consume **Free Float** without delaying any successor activities.

A Start to Finish relationship will drag a successor in front of it and act like a **Zero Float** constraint, but the use of this relationship is usually considered bad practice.

The Primavera **As Late As Possible** constraint calculates as a **Zero Free** constraint, it consumes Free Float not Total Float and will not delay any successor activities. This is not as a Microsoft Project **As Late As Possible** constraint which consumes Total Float and will delay successor tasks.

4 INTERESTING FEATURES

4.1 Wildcard Filters for Text Searching

The **Wildcard** functions are similar to the DOS Wildcard functions and are mainly used for filtering text:

- ❖ You may replace a single character with a "?". Thus, a filter searching for a word containing "b?t" will display words like "bat", "bit" and "but."
- ❖ The function is not case sensitive.
- ❖ You may replace a group of characters with an "*". Thus, a filter searching for a word containing "b*t" will display "blot", "blight" and "but."

Note: For the Wildcard function to operate the "**equals**" Test must be used. This function does not work with the "**contains**" and in this mode "**equals**" works as a "**contains**" operand, see the picture below which will find any task with **bid** or **bud** in the task name.

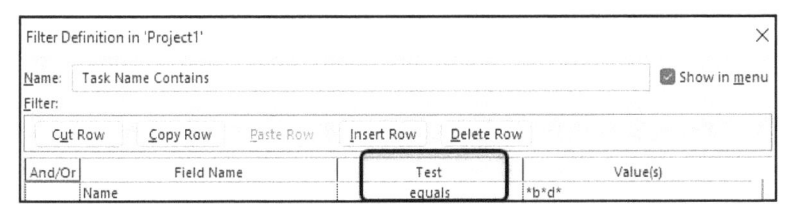

And/Or	Field Name	Test	Value(s)
	Name	equals	*b*d*

- ❖ **NA** allows the selection of a blank value. The filter below displays tasks without either a **Baseline Start** or **Baseline Finish** date:

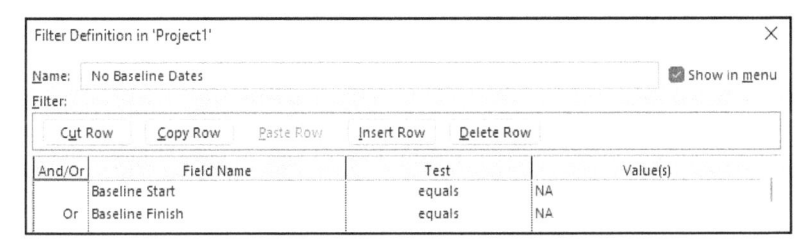

And/Or	Field Name	Test	Value(s)
	Baseline Start	equals	NA
Or	Baseline Finish	equals	NA

4.2 Interactive Filters

These filters allow you to enter a range of **Values** after applying the filter. Thus, filter is tailored each time it is applied via a user-prompt. The filter below will ask you to enter a range of dates. This filter is very useful to look at a time slice of activities and would be used to create a **Look Ahead** filter when updating a schedule.

For this function to operate properly, the text in the **Value(s)** field must commence with a double quote and end with a double quote and question mark, e.g. the format should be **"Question"?**. The text is user defined and may be any relevant text:

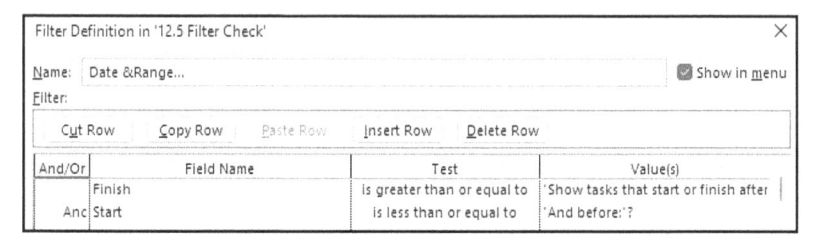

Filter Definition in '12.5 Filter Check'			
Name: Date &Range...			☑ Show in menu
Filter:			
Cut Row	Copy Row Paste Row	Insert Row Delete Row	
And/Or	Field Name	Test	Value(s)
	Finish	is greater than or equal to	"Show tasks that start or finish after
And	Start	is less than or equal to	'And before:'?

4.3 AutoFilters

AutoFilters are turned on by clicking on the ▼ button. They may be used to:

❖ **Filtering** tasks by either using the check boxes in the lower section or selecting from the options under the Filters option

❖ **Sort** is used to sort on a selected data item, but this also jumbles up the Summary Tasks,

❖ **Group** is used to Group tasks by the select data field. This only allows a single level of grouping. Use the **Group by:** function if the tasks are grouped by more than one field.

99 TRICKS & TRAPS FOR MICROSOFT PROJECT 2021 and 365

The picture below displays some of the options found with **AutoFilters** function:

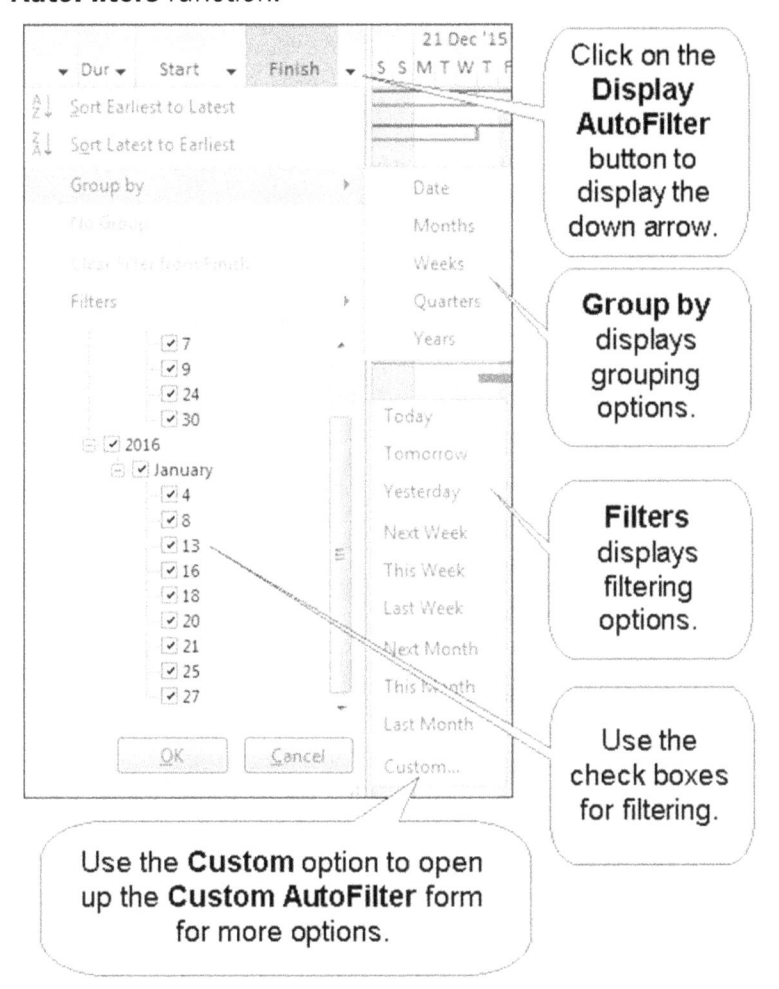

- Click on the **Display AutoFilter** button to display the down arrow.
- **Group by** displays grouping options.
- **Filters** displays filtering options.
- Use the check boxes for filtering.
- Use the **Custom** option to open up the **Custom AutoFilter** form for more options.

Note: AutoFilters will always show Summary Tasks.

4.4 Selecting Dates

There was a slick way of selecting dates in date fields in 2000 to 2003 by scrolling through days, months and years but this function was eliminated in 2007 and there were no improvements in versions 2010, 2013, 2016 or 2019.

In 2010 and later a calendar form is displayed by clicking on a date cell with the mouse pointer:

- ❖ To change the day, click on the required day.
- ❖ To select today's date, click on the Today button.
- ❖ To change the month and/or year; scroll a month at a time by clicking on the arrows on the top left-hand or top right-hand side of the form;

Click on the arrows to scroll through months and years

Note: When a date is selected from a column, Microsoft Project will set a constraint without informing the user. This may result in unintentionally setting a constraint.

4.5 Understanding Start and Finish Milestones

A Milestone is created by assigning a task a zero duration:

- ❖ A Milestone is a **Start Milestone** when it has no predecessors, see Task 1 below.
- ❖ A **Start Milestone** is at the start of a Time Period, for example, 8:00 am, see Task 1 below.
- ❖ A Milestone is a **Finish Milestone** if it has one or more predecessors, see Task 3 and 5 below.

- ❖ A **Finish Milestone** is at the end of a Time Period, for example, 5:00 pm, see Task 3 and 5 below.

	Task Name	Dur	Start	Finish	Predecessor
1	Start MS	0d	Tue 08:00 AM	Tue 08:00 AM	
2	Task	2d	Tue 08:00 AM	Wed 05:00 PM	1
3	Finish MS	0d	Wed 05:00 PM	Wed 05:00 PM	2
4	Task	1d	Thu 08:00 AM	Thu 05:00 PM	3
5	Finish MS	0d	Thu 05:00 PM	Thu 05:00 PM	4

- ❖ A task may also be made to look like a Milestone by checking the **Mark as a milestone** in the **Task Information** form **Advanced** tab, see Task 2 below.
- ❖ The task made to look like a Milestone may be set to display at the Start or Finish of the Tasks by editing the From and To fields of Milestones in the **Bar Styles** form:

Dur	Start	Finish
6d	Aug 5	Aug 11
3d	Aug 11	Aug 14
4d	Aug 14	Aug 18

Note:

- ❖ Unlike some other scheduling software, it is not possible for the user to assign a Milestone as either a Start or Finish Milestone in Microsoft Project. Also ensure your Milestone description matches the purpose of the Milestone; for example, a Finish Milestone would have "Completed" in the description.
- ❖ Milestones also ignore the assigned calendars and will be scheduled immediately after any predecessor:

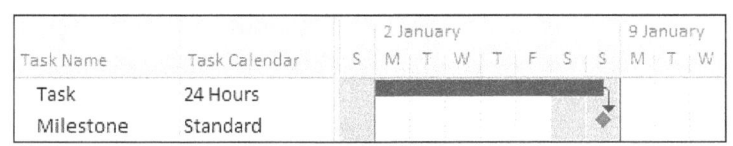

Task Name	Task Calendar
Task	24 Hours
Milestone	Standard

4.6 Converting a Finish Milestone into a Start Milestone

Sometimes it is important to have a Start Milestone that has a predecessor. For example, Task 5 in the picture below may be required on Friday morning not Thursday afternoon:

	Task Name	Dur	Start	Finish	Predecessor	August 4 M T W T F S
1	Start MS	0d	Tue 08:00	Tue 08:00		
2	Task	2d	Tue 08:00	Wed 17:00	1	
3	Finish MS	0d	Wed 17:00	Wed 17:00	2	
4	Task	1d	Thu 08:00	Thu 17:00	3	
5	Finish MS	0mins	Thu 17:00	Thu 17:00	4	
6	Task	1d	Fri 08:00	Fri 17:00	5	

One workaround to achieve this:

❖ Assign a short duration to the Start Milestone. The duration is not important, say 1 min.

❖ Check the **Mark as a Milestone** in the **General** tab of the **Task Information** form.

❖ Ensure all successors of the Start Milestone are Start to Start, otherwise all successors will span 1 day longer than their assigned duration:

➢ Without a Start to Start successor:

	Task Name	Dur	Start	Finish	Predecessor	4 August 11 W T F S S M T W
4	Task	1d	Thu 08:00	Thu 17:00	3	
5	Finish MS	1min	Fri 08:00	Fri 08:01	4	
6	Task	1d	Fri 08:01	Mon 08:01	5	

➢ With a Start to Start successor:

	Task Name	Dur	Start	Finish	Predecessor	4 August 11 W T F S S M T W
4	Task	1d	Thu 08:00	Thu 17:00	3	
5	Finish MS	1min	Fri 08:00	Fri 08:01	4	
6	Task	1d	Fri 08:00	Fri 17:00	5SS	

4.7 Creating a Hammock or a LEO Task

A **Hammock** or **Level Of Effort** (**LOE**) task is defined as a task that spans between two tasks or milestones and will change in duration when either of the driving dates change.

This is not a Summary Task created by Outlining and is not a Microsoft Project function but one may be created by:

- ❖ Assigning a Task Type that must not be **Fixed Duration** otherwise the duration will not change,
- ❖ A relationship is created between Start date of the driving Start milestone or Task and Hammock Start date using the **Copy Cell...** and **Paste Special...**, **Paste Link...** link command,
- ❖ Then a relationship is created between Finish date of the driving Finish Milestone or Task and Hammock Finish date using the **Copy Cell...** and **Edit**, **Paste Special...**, **Paste Link...** command.
- ❖ As either of the Driving milestones or tasks is moved the Hammock will recalculate its duration.

	Task Name	Dur	Start	Finish
1	Hammock	5d	Aug 6	Aug 12
2	Driving Start Task	1d	Aug 6	Aug 6
3	Driving Finish Milestone	0d	Aug 12	Aug 12

- ❖ In the picture above there has been a link created between the Start dates of Task 2 and Task 1 and the Finish dates of Task 3 and Task 1.

Note: A linked cell has triangle in the bottom right hand corner: 8 May

4.8 Elapsed Durations, Leads and Lags

4.8.1 Elapsed Durations

If you assign a task an **Elapsed** duration, the task will ignore all calendars and will be scheduled 24 hours a day and 7 days per week. To enter an elapsed duration, type an "**e**" between the duration and units.

- ❖ This is useful for tasks such as curing concrete or computer processes running 24 hours per day.
- ❖ The Total Float will calculate approximately three times longer than a task on an 8-hour per day calendar (depending on the length of the lunch break) and this may be misleading.

The example below shows the difference between a 7-**Elapsed Day** task and a 7-day task on a **Standard** (5-day per week) calendar.

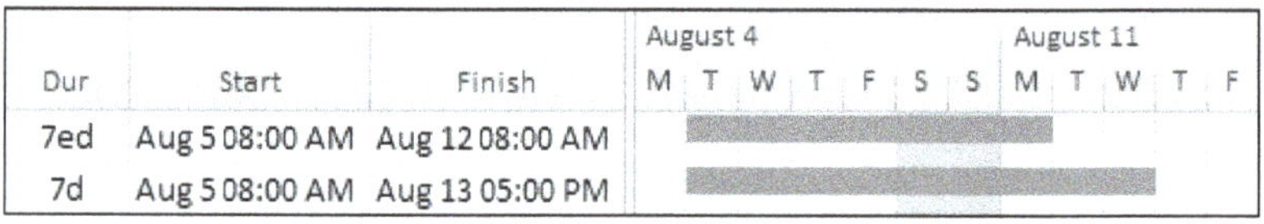

Dur	Start	Finish	August 4 M T W T F S S	August 11 M T W T F
7ed	Aug 5 08:00 AM	Aug 12 08:00 AM		
7d	Aug 5 08:00 AM	Aug 13 05:00 PM		

4.8.2 Float on Tasks with Elapsed Durations

The Float on Elapsed Duration tasks is calculated on a 24-hour per day calendar and will be different than a task on an 8-hour per day calendar:

Dur	Total Slack	August 4 M T W T F S S	August 11 M T W T F S S	August 18 M T W T F
12d	0d			
5ed	11ed			
5d	7d			

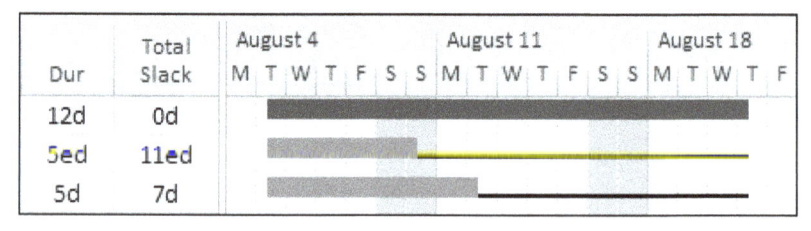

4.8.3 Elapsed Leads and Lags

An elapsed lead or lag may also be assigned to relationships and these also ignore all calendars:

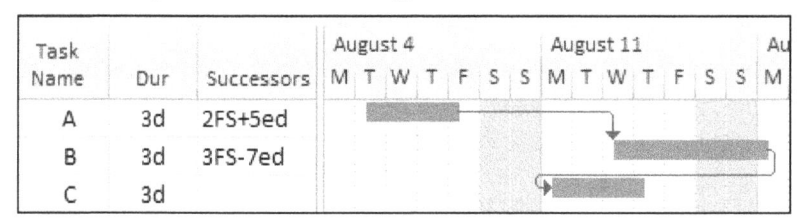

Task Name	Dur	Successors
A	3d	2FS+5ed
B	3d	3FS-7ed
C	3d	

4.9 Establishing Two Relationships between Two Tasks

Sometimes it is desirable to put two relationships between two activities, for example, a Start to Start and a Finish to Finish. This is often referred to as "Ladder Scheduling". It is not possible to put two relationships between two tasks in Microsoft Project unless a Milestone is inserted in the loop:

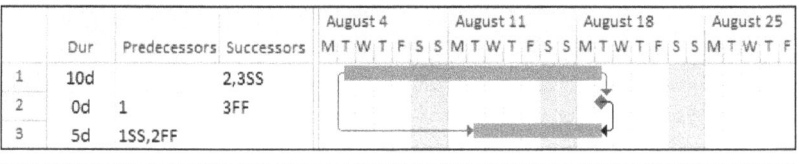

	Dur	Predecessors	Successors
1	10d		2,3SS
2	0d	1	3FF
3	5d	1SS,2FF	

	Dur	Predecessors	Successors
1	10d		2,3SS
2	0d	1	3FF
3	15d	1SS,2FF	

Note: Task 3 in the upper picture above has been dragged As Late As Possible by the Finish to Finish relationship.

4.10 Ladder scheduling

Large negative lags are normally unacceptable and Ladder Scheduling is used to link a set of tasks that have substantial overlap, such as pipe laying operations.

Most products allow multiple relationships between two tasks, as per the P6 example below, where the tasks are linked using two relationships, a SS+3d and a FF+3d:

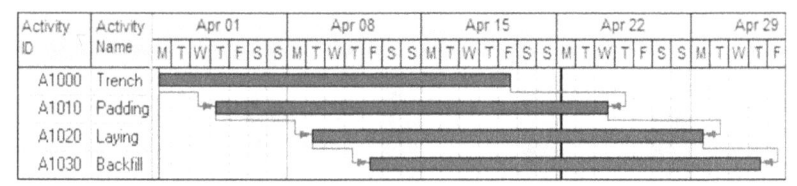

Activity ID	Activity Name	Apr 01	Apr 08	Apr 15	Apr 22	Apr 29
A1000	Trench					
A1010	Padding					
A1020	Laying					
A1030	Backfill					

Microsoft Project does not allow two relationships between tasks. Ladder Scheduling may be achieved by:

❖ Commencing a chain with a Start Milestone,
❖ Connect the Start Milestone to each task with a Start to Start plus the appropriate lag and
❖ Connect each task to their successor with a Finish to Finish relationship plus the appropriate lag:

	Task Name	Predecessors	Successors
1	Start pipe		2,3FS+3d,4FS+6d,5FS+9d
2	Trench	1	3FF+3d
3	Padding	1FS+3d,2FF+3d	4FF+3d
4	Laying	1FS+6d,3FF+3d	5FF+3d
5	Backfill	1FS+9d,4FF+3d	

4.11 % Lags

A **Percentage Lag** which may be typed into a Lag cell increases the Lag duration as the predecessor duration increases:

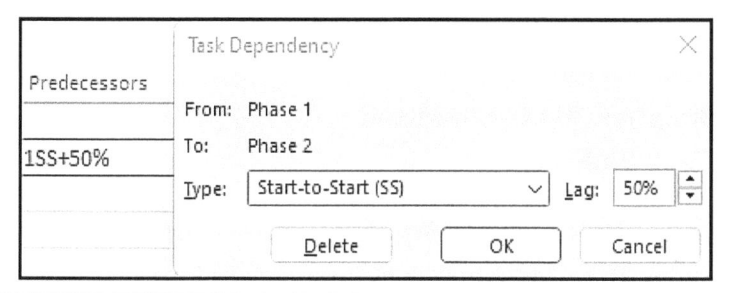

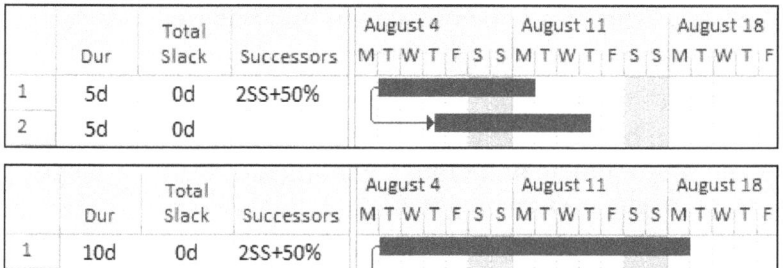

	Predecessors
1	
2	1SS+50%

Task Dependency

From: Phase 1
To: Phase 2
Type: Start-to-Start (SS)   Lag: 50%

	Dur	Total Slack	Successors	August 4 … August 18
1	5d	0d	2SS+50%	
2	5d	0d		

	Dur	Total Slack	Successors	August 4 … August 18
1	10d	0d	2SS+50%	
2	5d	0d		

The lag duration is calculated on the **Successor Calendar**. When the successor task is changed from an 8-hour per day calendar to a 24-hour per day calendar, the elapsed duration of the successor is reduced, as well as the elapsed duration of the lag. Now the Float is calculated on a 24-hour per day basis. Things get a bit tricky here!

	Dur	Total Slack	Successors	August 4 … August 18
1	5d	0d	2SS+50%	
2	5d	11.63d		

Note: Microsoft Project 2000 calculated the lag on the Project Calendar.

4.12 Tracing Logic

Sometimes it is difficult to trace logic in a complex project with relationships flying up and down a Gantt Chart.

There are some tools you may consider using to resolve these issues including:

- **Task Drivers**
- **Relationship Diagram** and
- **Task Path**

4.12.1 Task Drivers and Task Inspector

A **Driving Relationship** is the predecessor that determines the Early Start of a non-critical task that has two predecessors which have different finish dates.

Microsoft Project 2000–2003 does not identify the difference between **Driving** and **Non-driving Relationships**, which often makes analyzing a schedule difficult. In these earlier versions of Microsoft Project, the simplest way to determine the driving relationship for tasks not on the critical path and with more than one predecessor was to delete the relationships until the task moved.

Microsoft Project 2007 introduced a **Task Drivers** form that indicates the driving predecessor and whether the schedule has been Resource Leveled. It also displays the effects of leveling. This was renamed **Task Inspector** in Microsoft Project 2013.

99 TRICKS & TRAPS FOR MICROSOFT PROJECT 2021 and 365

In Microsoft Project 365, 2021, 2019, 2016 and 2013, go to **Task**, **Tasks** group and from the drop down menu contained in **Inspect**, select the **Inspect** button to open the **Inspector** pane, which displays information as in the picture below:

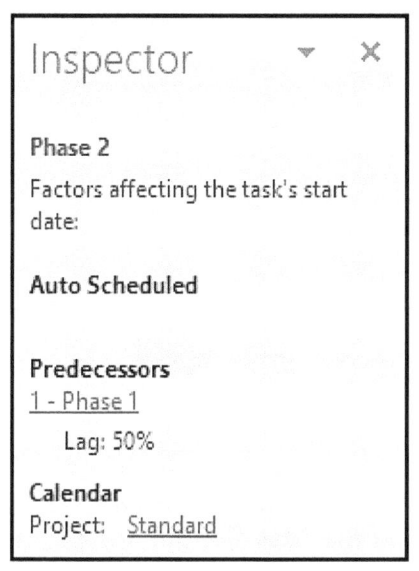

```
Inspector                      ▼  ✕

Phase 2
Factors affecting the task's start
date:

Auto Scheduled

Predecessors
1 - Phase 1
     Lag: 50%

Calendar
Project:  Standard
```

In order to see the **Driving Predecessors** and/or **Driving Successors**, click on the ⬚ **Task Path** icon located on the **Gantt Chart Format** toolbar:

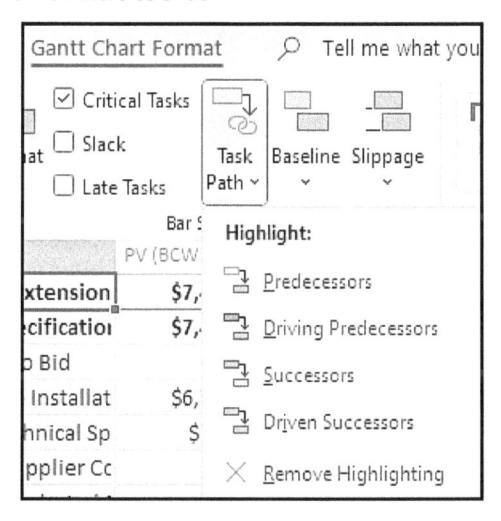

```
Gantt Chart Format        🔍  Tell me what you

  ☑ Critical Tasks
  ☐ Slack           Task   Baseline  Slippage
  ☐ Late Tasks      Path ⌄

              Bar    Highlight:
              PV (BCW
xtension      $7,      Predecessors
cification    $7,      Driving Predecessors
 Bid                   Successors
 Installat    $6,
nical Sp      $        Driven Successors
pplier Cc              ✕  Remove Highlighting
```

4.12.2 Tracing the Logic

Another method to trace the logic is to display the **Bar Chart** in the Top Pane and the **Relationship Diagram** in the Bottom Pane. Scroll up and down in the Gantt Chart to identify the predecessors and successors:

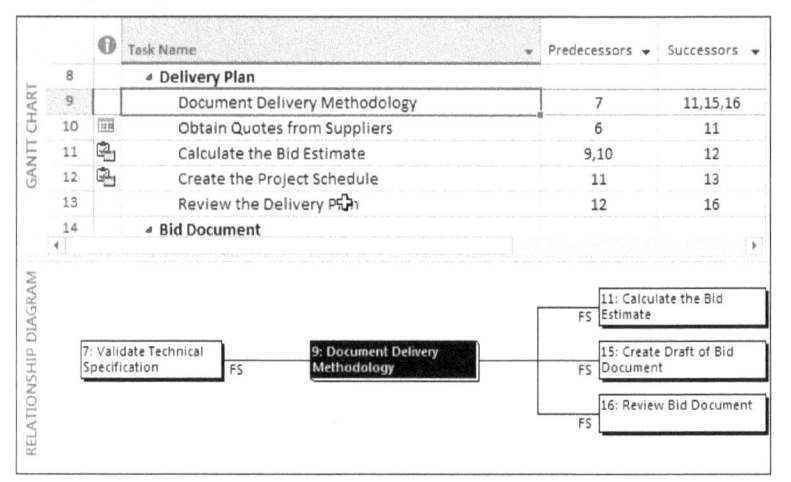

Another method is to display the **Relationship Diagram** in the Top Pane and the **Task Form** in the Bottom Pane. Click on the predecessors or successors in the Relationship Diagram to follow the logic:

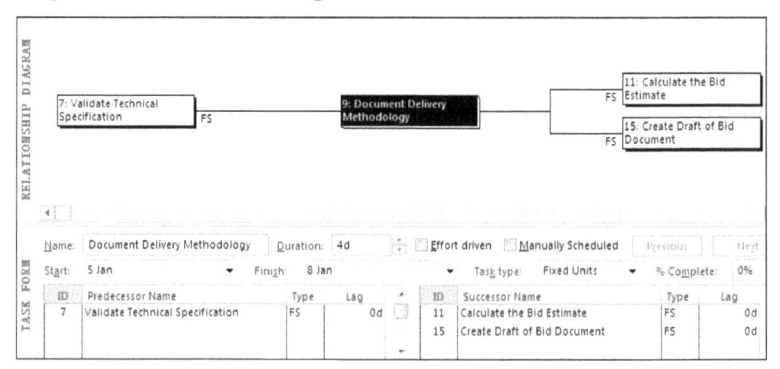

4.12.3 Finding a Chain of Driving Predecessors of Successors – Displaying the Task Path

Microsoft Project 2013 introduced a function titled **Task Path** found by selecting **Gantt Chart Format**, **Bar Styles**, **Task Path** and selecting one of the options.

This function will highlight the tasks that match the criteria in the colors indicated on the menu.

You may need to turn of the Critical Path highlighting for this to display correctly.

4.12.4 Finding Tasks with Lags

To find any task that has a predecessor or successor with a lag you should create a filter as per the picture below, the **Values** are a "+" and a "-":

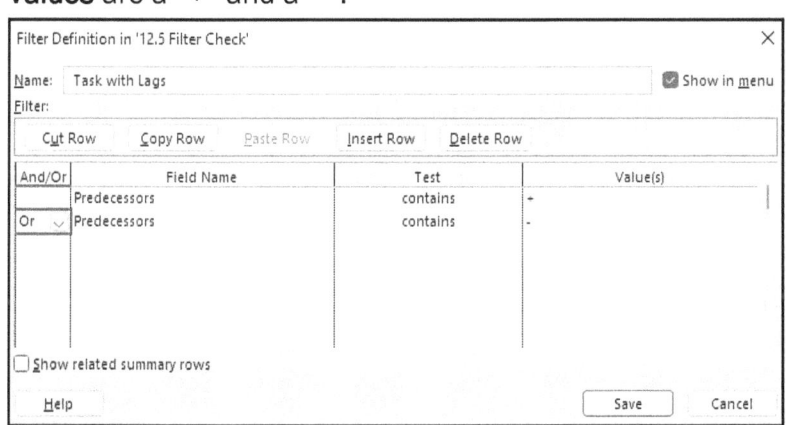

5 MAKING IT LOOK RIGHT

5.1 Date Format Dangers

There is often confusion on international projects between the numerical US date style (mmddyy) and the numerical European date style (ddmmyy). For example, in the United States 020719 is read as 07 Feb '19, and in many other countries as 02 Jul '19. Consider adopting the ddmmmyy style, **06 Jan '09** or mmmddyy style, **Jan 06 '09** to avoid expensive litigation when dates are misunderstood.

Select **File, Options** to display the **Options** form and select the **General** tab **Date format:**:

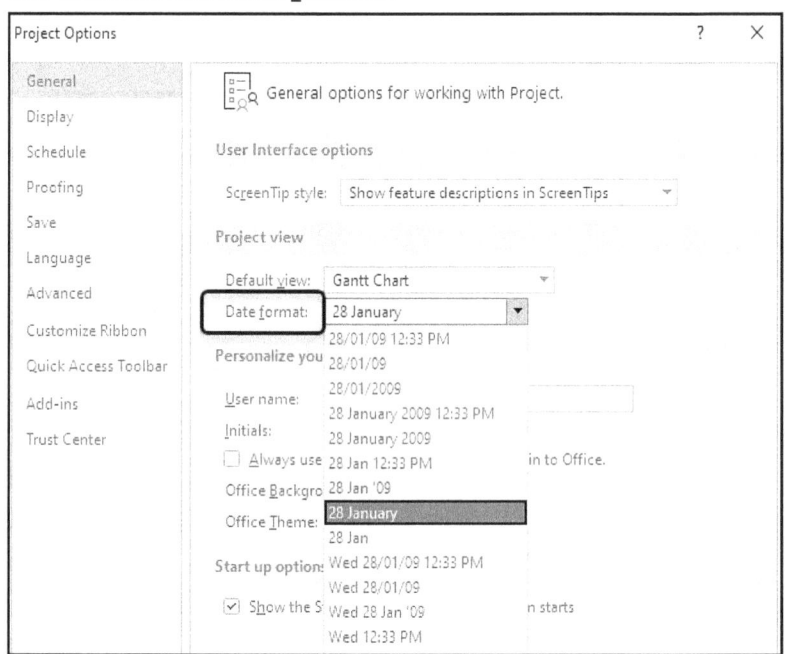

This option selects the display style of the dates for all projects. The date format options available will be dependent on your system default settings. You may adjust your system date format under the **Control Panel**, **Regional and Language Options**.

5.2 Preventing the Date Format from Changing on Other Computers

The date format selected in the **File, Options, General** tab applies to all projects opened on one computer. Some projects may be required to display the day and time format and others day and month, so you have to keep changing the format each time you open a different project.

If you are in this situation, you may override the date format selected in the **File, Options, General** tab by a date format selected in a **View**, **Data**, **Tables**, **More Tables...** form:

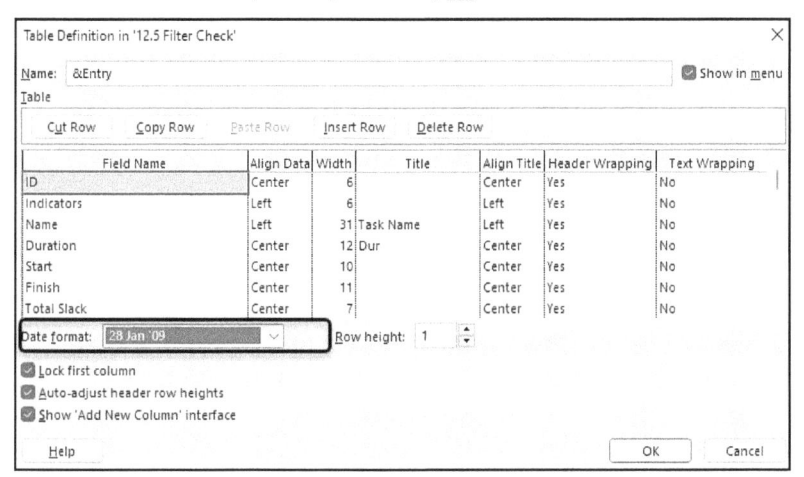

Each project could have its own set of tables all with their own project-specific date format.

When you send this project to someone else, they will have a better chance of seeing the same date format as you especially if their **Control Panel**, **Regional and Language Options** are the same as yours.

5.3 The Smart Way to Create Views

A single Gantt Chart View is made from a Gantt Screen and includes a Table, an optional Group and an optional Filter. A View also holds the Bar formatting and Print settings.

If your project requires multiple but similar Views, for example, headers and footers may need to contain the same print settings and bar formatting consistent, then the following process is recommended:

- ❖ Each View should have a unique name. This name should be used for the Table, Group and Filter names associated with the View, so each view has its own unique Table, Filter and Group with the same name.
- ❖ Create the Tables, Filters and Groups for each View.
- ❖ Create the first View and make sure the Bar formatting and the Print settings are correct.
- ❖ The uniquely named Tables, Groups and Filters should not be displayed in the menus to avoid their inadvertent application and corruption.
- ❖ The print preview Header, Footer and Legend should read all the text data from the **File**, **Info**, **Project Information**, **Advanced Properties** form. Thus, a change to the header or footer text can be made in one place for all Views, the **File**, **Info**, **Project Information**, **Advanced Properties** form.
- ❖ Ensure that you have hidden all the bars that you do not want displayed in the Legend, by placing an "*****" in front of the bar name in the **Bars** form. See Para 6.5.
- ❖ Create new Views by copying the first View only after it has been checked, double-checked, and checked again.

5.4 Bar Formatting

Select **Gantt Chart Format**, **Format**, **Layout** to open the **Layout** form, which has some interesting features:

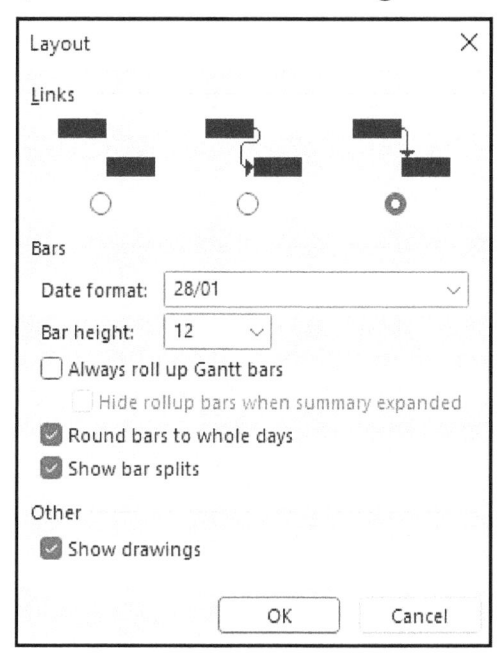

5.4.1 Bar Date Format

The **Bar Date format** option sets the format for dates displayed on bars only.

The option to display dates on:

❖ One or more selected bars is made using the **Gantt Chart Format**, **Bar Styles**, **Format**, **Bar** or

❖ On all bars with the **Gantt Chart Format**, **Bar Styles**, **Format**, **Bar Styles** form.

5.4.2 Bar Heights

The **Bar height:** option sets the height of all the bars.

Individual bars may be assigned different heights by selecting a bar shape in the styles form.

5.4.3 Always Roll Up Gantt Bars

Always roll up Gantt bars and **Hide rollup bars when summary expanded** works as follows:

❖ Tasks before roll up:

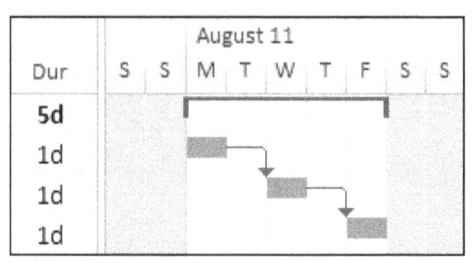

	August 11
Dur	S S M T W T F S S
5d	
1d	
1d	
1d	

❖ Tasks with **Always roll up Gantt bars** checked and **Hide rollup bars when summary expanded** unchecked, results in both Summary and Detailed tasks displayed in the Bar Chart when rolled up:

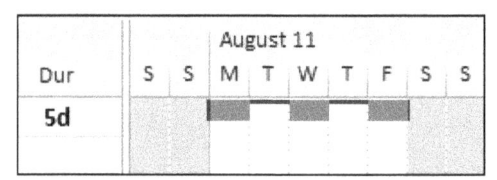

	August 11
Dur	S S M T W T F S S
5d	

❖ Tasks with both **Always roll up Gantt bars** and **Hide rollup bars when summary expanded** checked, results in the Summary Task bar being hidden when the Detailed Tasks are rolled up:

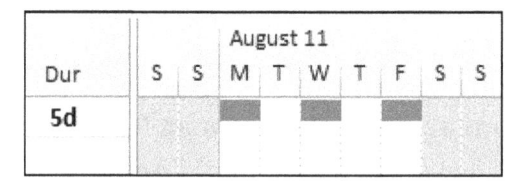

	August 11
Dur	S S M T W T F S S
5d	

- An individual bar may be rolled up to a summary task using the **Rollup** option in the **Task Information** form, **General** tab when **Always roll up Gantt bars** options are unchecked.

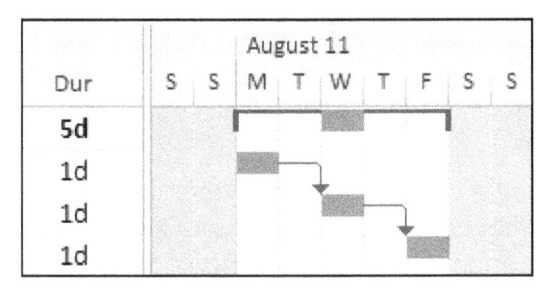

Dur	August 11
	S S M T W T F S S
5d	
1d	
1d	
1d	

5.4.4 Round Bars to Whole Days

The **Round bars to whole days:** is used to make it easier to see short duration bars on a long duration schedule:

- When this option is unchecked, the length of the task will be shown in proportion to the total number of hours worked per day over the 24-hour time span. For example, an 8-hour working duration bar is shown below:

Dur	August 11
	M T W T F
1d	

- When this option is checked, the task bar is often displayed and spanned over the whole day irrespective of calendar working time:

Dur	August 11
	M T W T F
1d	

5.5 Putting Text on Bars

5.5.1 Placing a Single Field on Bars

A single field may be placed on all bars using the **Gantt Chart Format**, **Bar Styles**, **Format**, **Bar** form or selected bars using the **Gantt Chart Format**, **Bar Styles**, **Format**, **Bar Styles** form and the **Font Size** is specified in the **Text Styles** form.

When adding a single field to all bars it is best to avoid adding the field to multiple bars because it is time consuming and takes a long time to remove the text.

It is better to create a single bar that does not display any bar formatting (a blank bar) and adding the Text field to this bar:

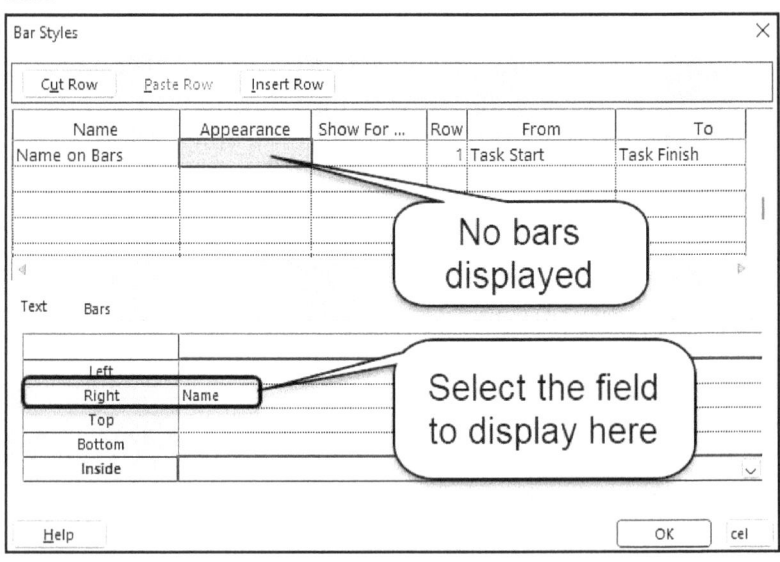

Note: The length of the Bar Chart may be reduced by placing the text on top of the bar instead of the end:

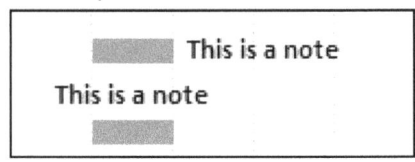

5.6 Placing Multiple Fields in a single position on a Bar

To place multiple Fields in a single position on a bar, such as the Start, Duration and Finish, then you should use a Text Field and concatenate the three existing fields in the Text Field:

- ❖ Open the **Custom Fields** form,
- ❖ Rename a Text field using the **Rename** button,
- ❖ Click on the **Formula** button and concatenate the fields using the "&" sign,
- ❖ The duration is held in minutes and has to be divided by 8 hours and 60 minutes and
- ❖ Text such as the "d," are added with inverted commas at the start and end of the text

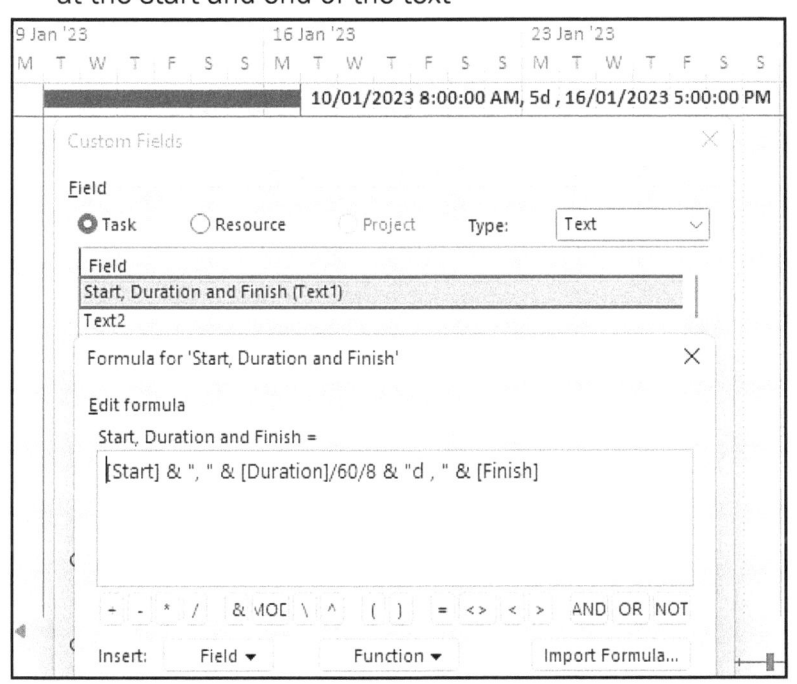

5.7 Format Colors

Colors are formatted in a number of forms:

- **Nonworking time** colors in the Gantt Chart are formatted in the **Timescale** form; double-click on the timescale.
- **Text** colors are formatted in the **Gantt Chart Format**, **Format**, **Text Styles** and **Font** forms.
- **Gridline** colors are formatted in the **Gantt Chart Format**, **Format**, **Gridlines** form.
- **Hyperlink** colors are formatted under **File, Options, Advanced** tab.
- **Timescale** and **Column Header** colors are formatted with the system color scheme selected from the **File, Options, General, Office Theme**.
- The **Logic Lines**, also known as **Dependencies**, **Relationships**, or **Links**, inherit their color from the predecessor's bar color in the Gantt Chart view and may be formatted in the Network Diagram view by selecting **Gantt Chart Format**, **Format**, **Layout** form.

5.8 How to Stop Text Wrapping

Many people get frustrated with the way Microsoft Project seems to wrap text without warning when columns are adjusted in width and clicking on the **Wrap Text** button does not solve the problem.

The field that controls the wrapping of text is the **Text Wrapping** field found in the **View, Data, Tables, More Tables** form and selecting a **Table** to edit:

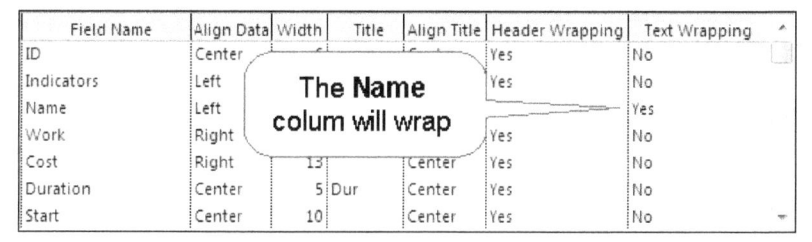

Field Name	Align Data	Width	Title	Align Title	Header Wrapping	Text Wrapping
ID	Center				Yes	No
Indicators	Left				Yes	No
Name	Left		The **Name** colum will wrap			Yes
Work	Right				Yes	No
Cost	Right	13		Center	Yes	No
Duration	Center	5	Dur	Center	Yes	No
Start	Center	10		Center	Yes	No

To stop ALL Text Wrapping you either:

❖ Open the **Tables** form and set all columns to No in the **Text Wrapping** field, or

❖ If you wish to use the **Wrap Text** button then you must select the column first, then click on the **Wrap Text** button and the readjust the row heights by selecting the **Select All** button and adjusting one row.

		Name	Work	Cost
1		Bid For Fa...	hrs	$59,260.00
2		▲ Techn...	rs	$24,000.00
3	✓	App...	rs	$0.00
4	✓	Dete...	hrs	$5,040.00
5		Create Technical Spe	96hrs	$14,480.00
6		Identify Supplier Cor	16hrs	$1,120.00

This is the Select All button.

5.9 Text direction options

This was new to Version 2021 and allowed the direction of text in some forms to be displayed Left-to-right (LTR) as in most European languages or Right-to-left (RTL) as in some Middle Eastern and Asian languages like Arabic, Hebrew, Persian, and Urdu.

The text in Organizer form below is aligned RTL:

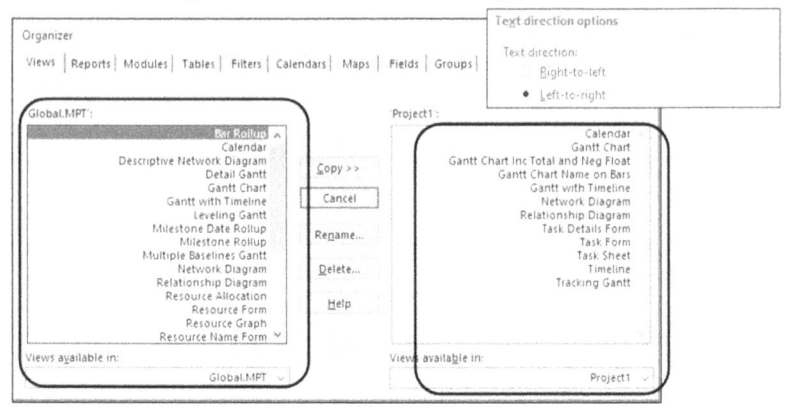

5.10 Display Tasks without Successors as Critical

Normally a task that does not have successors will display Float, as per task 4 below:

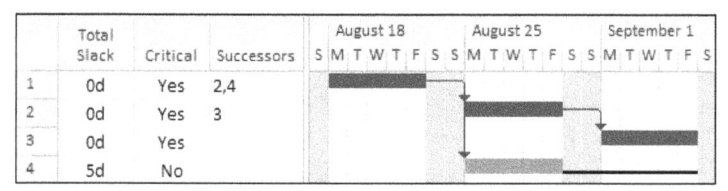

	Total Slack	Critical	Successors
1	0d	Yes	2,4
2	0d	Yes	3
3	0d	Yes	
4	5d	No	

❖ Select the **File**, **Options**, **Advanced** tab, **Calculation options for this project:** section,

❖ Check the **Calculate multiple critical paths** box and then tasks:

  ➢ Without successors will have their Late dates set to equal their Early dates and will be calculated with zero Total Float (Slack),
  ➢ Displayed as critical in the bar chart and
  ➢ Are indicated critical in the Critical column.

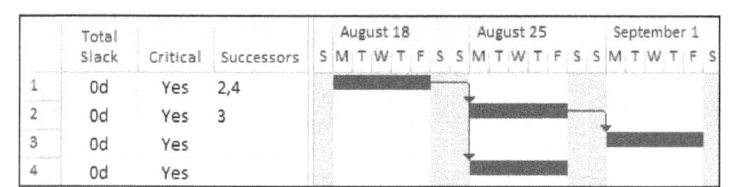

	Total Slack	Critical	Successors
1	0d	Yes	2,4
2	0d	Yes	3
3	0d	Yes	
4	0d	Yes	

You might consider using this function when:

❖ You would like to display **Multiple Critical Paths**. This situation happens in a schedule with several areas of separable parts and you wish to display the critical path for each area, or

❖ You have few or no relationships in the schedule and you want to fool people into thinking that you have created a schedule where all tasks are on the critical path. In this situation, don't forget to hide the Indicators, Predecessor and Successor columns!

5.11 Preventing Descriptions from Indenting

When a project has a number of Summary Task levels and the task descriptions are long, then the Task Name column may have to be widened to display the full description:

#	Task Name	Duration
1	⊿ Bid for Facility Extension	36d
2	⊿ Technical Specification	14d
3	Determine Installation Requirements	3d
4	Create Technical Specification	12d
5	⊿ Delivery Plan	32d

To prevent the Task Name from indenting select the **File, Options, Quick Access Toolbar** tab, **Choose commands from: All commands**, select the **Indent Name** option and press **Add.** Go to the quick access toolbar and uncheck the box for **Indent name**:

#	Task Name	Duration
1	⊿ Bid for Facility Extension	36d
2	⊿ Technical Specification	14d
3	Determine Installation Requirements	3d
4	Create Technical Specification	12d
5	⊿ Delivery Plan	32d

Note: Small indents may be created by typing spaces at the start of the Task Names.

5.12 Reducing Column Widths

It is useful to reduce the width of columns so more data may be displayed on screen and in printouts. There are several ways to reduce column widths:

❖ To prevent the Task Name from indenting, go to the **Quick Access Toolbar** and uncheck the **Indent name** option. Refer to para 5.11 for instructions on how to add this command.

❖ To reduce the width of the **Duration** column, select the **File, Options, Advanced** tab and under **Display options for this project:**

  ➢ **Mi̱nutes:**, **H̱ours:**, **Day̱s:**, **W̱eeks:**, **Moṉths:**, **Y̱ears:** – From the drop-down boxes, select your preferred designators for these units. Change "days" to "d" and "hr" to "h" to make the duration columns narrower.

  ➢ **Add space before label** – Places a space between the value and the label; uncheck this to make duration columns narrower.

  ➢ Change the column title from Duration to Dur:

❖ Change the date format to a shorter format in the **File, Options, General** tab.

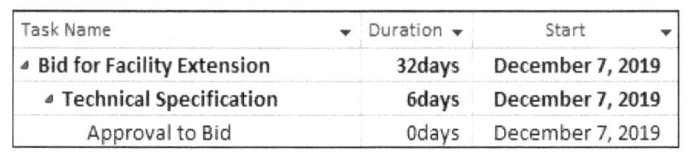

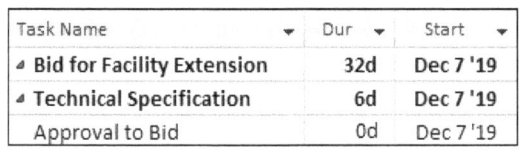

Task Name	Duration	Start
⊿ Bid for Facility Extension	32days	December 7, 2019
⊿ Technical Specification	6days	December 7, 2019
Approval to Bid	0days	December 7, 2019

Task Name	Dur	Start
⊿ Bid for Facility Extension	32d	Dec 7 '19
⊿ Technical Specification	6d	Dec 7 '19
Approval to Bid	0d	Dec 7 '19

5.13 How to Display a Task ID that Will Not Change

One frustrating part of using Microsoft Project is that the Task ID is not unique and as new tasks are inserted, then the ID changes. The Task ID is therefore a Line Number. The Unique ID field helps resolve this issue, which is often very important in dispute resolution. Each task is assigned a Unique ID when it is created. This number is not used again in the schedule, even if the task is deleted.

There are two other columns that may be used to edit and display relationships using the Unique ID:

- The **Unique ID Predecessor**, and
- The **Unique ID Successor**.

The Task **Unique ID** allows users to identify easily which activities have been added or deleted or when a revised schedule has been submitted.

On the other hand, if one wants to reset the Unique ID, or hide the addition or deletion of tasks, then create a new schedule, transfer the calendars, etc. with **Organizer**, and copy and paste all the resources and then tasks into the new schedule.

5.14 Hiding Task Information

Sometimes it is desirable to hide some information in a bar or cell about a specific task.

5.14.1 Hiding Bars

To hide a bar:
- ❖ Open Task Information from the General tab, and
- ❖ Check the Hide bar option.

5.14.2 Hiding Text

To hide text in one or more cells:
- ❖ Select the cells,
- ❖ Right Click and use the **Text Styles** function to make the Text color the same color as the Background, usually white.

5.14.3 Marking Tasks Inactive

To inactive function found on the **Task Information** form, **General** tab in Professional versions only makes a task inactive:
- ❖ This allows you to effectively remove a task from the schedule calculations,
- ❖ The pictures below show the before and after of making a task **Inactive**:

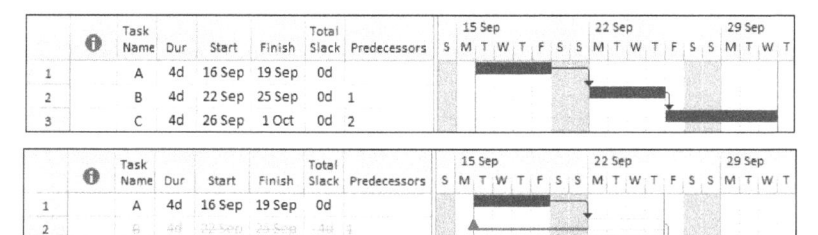

Note: This is useful to show scope being removed from a project but maintain a visible history and is only available in the Professional Versions and not the Standard Versions.

5.15 Anchor a Vertical Line to a Milestone

It is often useful to have a vertical line on the Bar Chart to show the end of a Phase or Stage that will move as the project is rescheduled.

- Insert a vertical line on the Bar Chart using the **Gantt Chart Format**, **Drawings**, **Drawing** function.
- Select the **Line** option and draw it on the screen.
- To attach the vertical line to a Task so it moves when the task moves:
- Double-click on the vertical line to open the **Format Drawing** form,
- Select the **Size & Position** tab and select the Task ID to attach the line and the relative position to the bar:

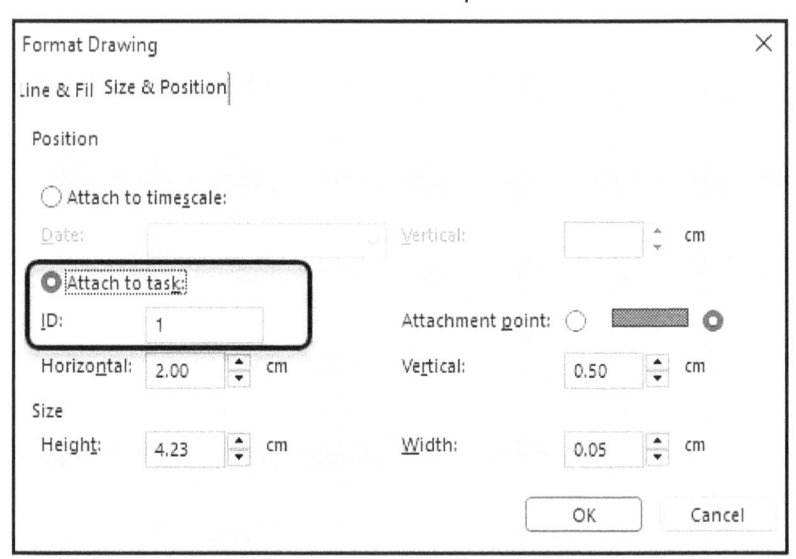

```
Format Drawing                                          X

Line & Fill  Size & Position

Position

○ Attach to timescale:
  Date:                    Vertical:              cm

● Attach to task:
  ID:    1                 Attachment point: ○  ■  ●
  Horizontal: 2.00  cm     Vertical:  0.50       cm

Size
  Height:  4.23   cm       Width:     0.05       cm

                                    OK      Cancel
```

5.16 Zoom Slider Dangers

The **Zoom Slider** was introduced with Microsoft Project 2010 and replaced the **View, Zoom...** function. This may be found at the bottom right-hand side of the screen and provides a simple way of scaling the time scale in the Gantt Chart and all other time scaled views such as the Calendar, Usage and Network Diagram View.

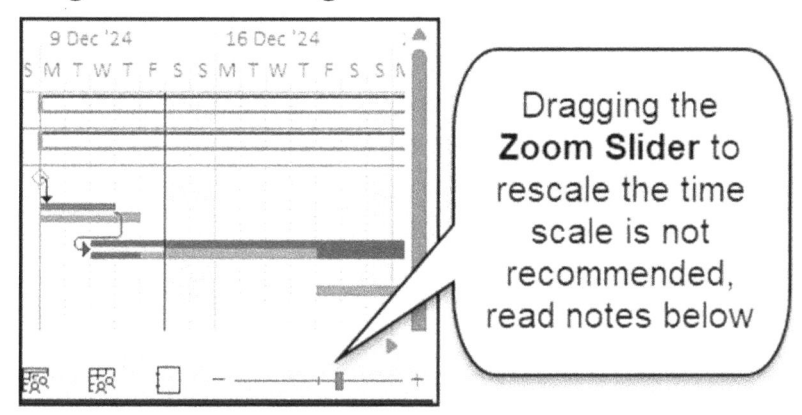

Dragging the **Zoom Slider** to rescale the time scale is not recommended, read notes below

This function works differently to other scheduling software in that it changes the scale and the displayed time units at the same time and may result in some undesirable time units being displayed, such as 3 and 11 day time intervals.

Once this function is used, your original timescale date formatting will be lost and may only be recovered with undo as this function applies its own formatting such as date formats.

The author has found that more predictable results are achieved by using the traditional **Zoom In** and **Zoom Out** functions which may be added to the Quick Access Toolbar.

There is a Quick Access Toolbar with all the commonly used commands available for downloaded from **www.eh.com.au** website **Software & Downloads** page.

Note: You may wish to remove the **Zoom Slider** from the Status bar at the bottom on the screen.

5.17 Why Is the Non-working Time Displayed Incorrectly?

The **Timescale** form provides a number of options for timescale display including the shading of **Nonworking** time.

To open the **Timescale** form Double-click on the timescale. The **Nonworking time** tab allows you to format how the nonworking time is displayed. You may select only one calendar. The nonworking time may be presented as shading behind the bars, in front of the bars or hidden.

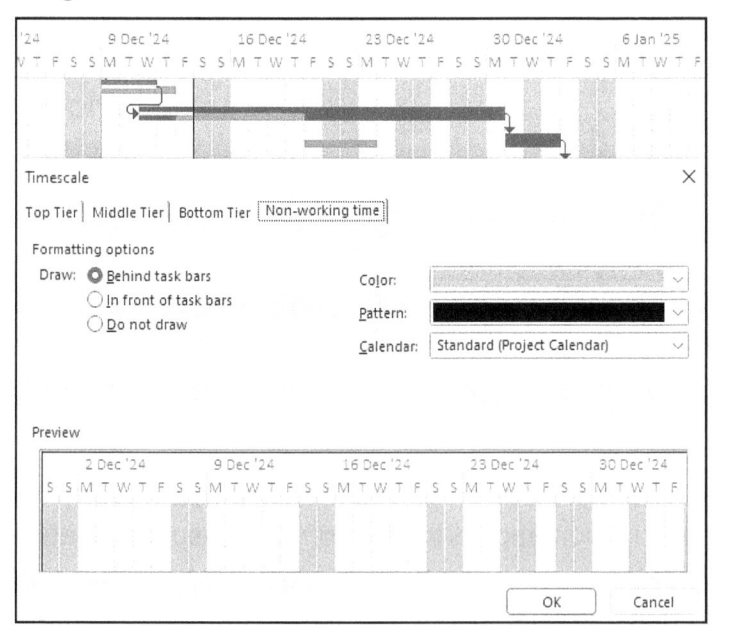

Notes:

By default, this is set to the Standard Calendar for each view and does not change when the Project Default Calendar is changed.

Therefore, if you change the Project Base calendar in the **Project Information** and you wish to see this new calendar in all views, then you will have to edit all the views.

5.18 Multiple Baseline Bar Display

Microsoft Project has the ability to record 11 baselines, but only provides the option to display one baseline bar and the **Variance Finish** column that is calculated from the **Baseline Finish** and **Finish** fields.

- Additional baselines may be set in the **Set Baseline** form,
- The first baseline bar may be displayed by using the **Format, Baseline Styles, Baseline** dropdown box,
- The additional baseline bars may be created by opening the **Bar Styles** form, cutting the existing Baseline bar and then pasting it twice.
- Then edit one of the baseline bars to suit the second baseline:

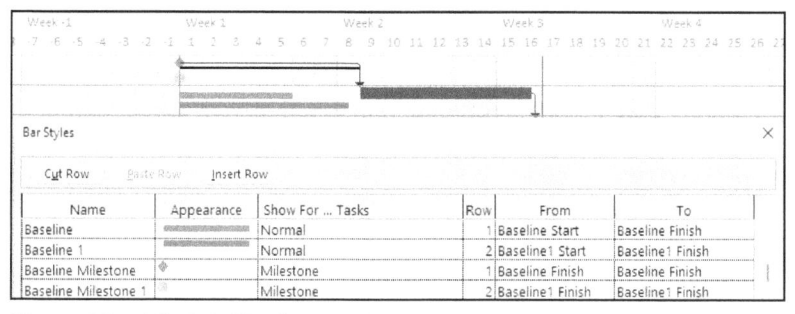

Name	Appearance	Show For ... Tasks	Row	From	To
Baseline		Normal	1	Baseline Start	Baseline Finish
Baseline 1		Normal	2	Baseline1 Start	Baseline1 Finish
Baseline Milestone		Milestone	1	Baseline Finish	Baseline Finish
Baseline Milestone 1		Milestone	2	Baseline1 Finish	Baseline1 Finish

Note: The **Finish Variance** field only operates on the **Baseline** fields and not **Baseline 1 to 10** fields. You may use a **Custom** field and formula to calculate **Baseline 1 to 10** field variances.

5.19 Ordinal Date Display

Often it is required to display ordinal dates in elapsed days, weeks or months from the start of a project.

This allows delays and extension of time to be seen in units other than the units used to display durations and the elapsed duration of a project to be evaluated.

This may be achieved in the **Timescale** form:

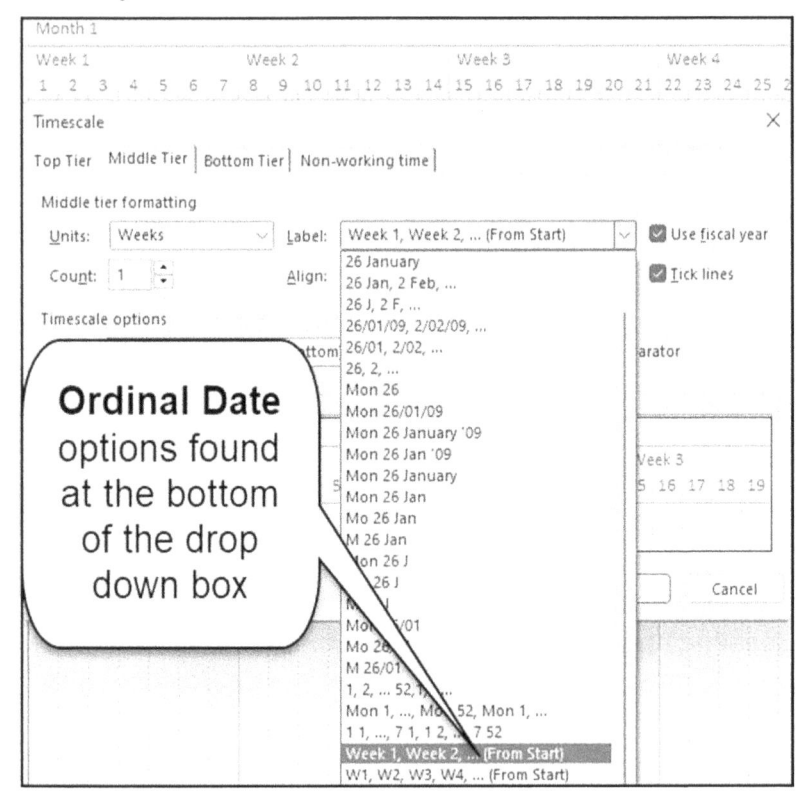

Ordinal Date options found at the bottom of the drop down box

5.20 Displaying an S-Curve

A single S-Curve may be created graphically and displayed by Microsoft Project by:

- Displaying the **Resource Sheet** in the top pane and selecting all the resources,
- The **Resource Graph** in the bottom pane,
- Right-clicking and displaying the **Cumulative Costs**, and
- Right-clicking, opening the **Bar Styles...** form and formatting as shown below:

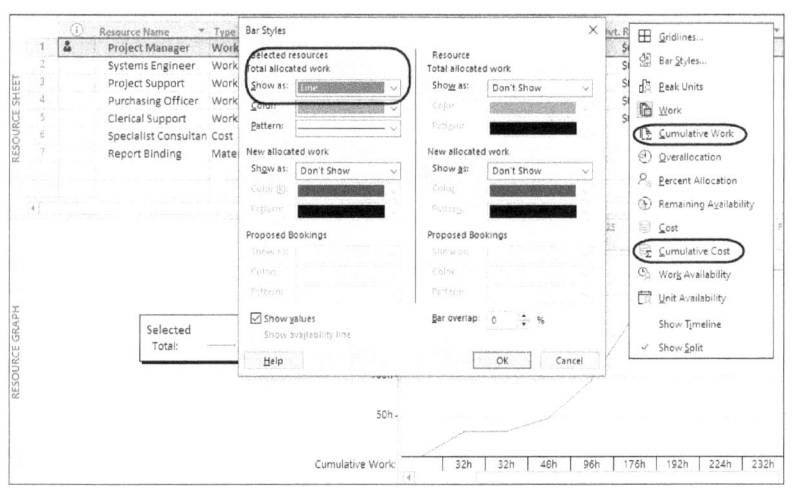

When more than one S-Curve is required, then it is suggested that the data should be exported to Excel with the **Report** toolbar, **Visual Reports** button and graphed, or you could consider using a product like **DecisionEdge**.

5.21 Displaying Cumulative Histogram

This may be achieved in a similar way as an S-Curve by:

❖ Selecting **Cumulative Work** and
❖ Selecting the **Bar** option in the **Bar Styles...** form under **Total allocated work** for **Selected resources**.

5.22 Displaying a Project Summary Task

A **Project Summary Task** may be displayed by checking the **Show project summary task** box from the **File**, **Options**, **Advanced** tab, **Display options for this project:** section.

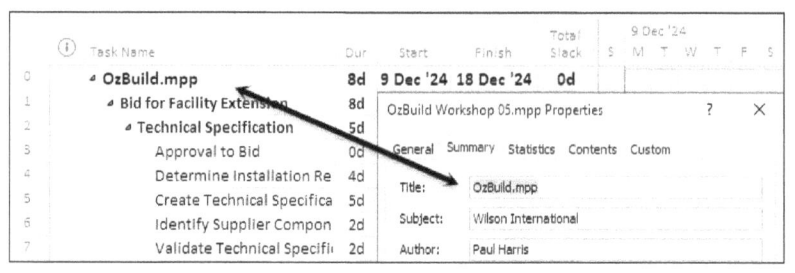

❖ This task spans from the first to the last task in the project and is, in effect, a built-in Level 0 **Outline Level** Task.
❖ The **Project Summary Task** description is linked to the **Project Title** in the **File**, **Project Information**, **Advanced Properties** form.
❖ A **Project Summary Task** is a virtual task and may not be assigned resources, relationships or constraints.

Note: Unfortunately, in some versions the **Project Title** in **Properties** form is linked to the file name the project is saved with and this link may not be broken, so the **Project Summary** task is then always the same as the **File Name**. As a result, I avoid using the **Title** in the **Properties** form.

6 GETTING IT OUT - PRINTING

6.1 Printing to One Page Wide

Printing in Microsoft Project has always been a little problematic and requires a little patience to get right, but the following suggestions may assist:

- ❖ Create Views that are just used for printing and once they work do not edit them or use them for day-to-day maintenance of the schedule.
- ❖ If you wish to fit a schedule to one page wide it is usually best to make sure that most of the schedule fits onto the screen, or at least that the columns and bars each do not occupy more than 2/3 of a typical a laptop screen.
- ❖ Try printing to a pdf writer with an A3 or 11" x 17" paper size and then reduce the paper size when printing to an A4 or Letter paper size.

To reduce the width of columns, as discussed earlier:

- ❖ Select a narrow date format,
- ❖ Select the **File, Options, Edit** tab and select a narrow format for the durations; for example, use "d" and not "days".
- ❖ Select the **File**, **Options, Advanced** tab and uncheck the **Add space before label** option. This will remove the space between the duration value and units.
- ❖ Consider increasing the row height so the Task Name column width may be reduced and text displayed on two or more lines.

6.2 Printing a Date Range

A date range may be selected from the **Print** form. In earlier versions of Microsoft Project, this had to be selected from the **File** menu, but in later versions these dates may be edited by selecting Print from the **Print Preview** form.

These dates are saved with the View so you may wish to consider creating a view for each date range.

In addition, a filter may be created to remove tasks that are not in the date range to be printed.

6.3 Printing a Gantt Chart and Resource Graph or Usage Table on One Page

Microsoft Project allows the display of a Gantt Chart in the Top Pane and a Resource Graph or Usage Table in the bottom pane but does not print the two panes in one printout.

- ❖ One option is to print both reports to a pdf writer and then use the pdf software to create one file with both pages. The Gantt Chart and Table or Histogram will not be on the same page but will be in one report. Programs like Adobe Acrobat enable this.
- ❖ Another option is to use a screen capture program like SnagIt and copy both the top and bottom pane to Excel or Word to create a combined report.

6.4 Printing the Calendar

It is always useful to be able to print out the calendar for people to review the working hours and non-work periods.

Microsoft has removed the old Reports from 2013 and therefore the ability to print a text **Working Days** report, which listed the **Non Work** days, has been lost. The options to print only the calendar are:

- ❖ Save your project, delete all tasks, display and print the **Calendar** view, or
- ❖ Download a third-party software that will print the calendars, such as Asta Powerproject, or
- ❖ Using a Screen Capture program like Snagit and Screen Capture pictures of the Calendar, a month at a time.

6.5 Hiding Unwanted Bars in the Legend

You will find a large number of bars are displayed in the **Legend** when printing and these are often undesirable in reports as they consume a lot of space at the bottom of the page.

These should not be deleted from the **Bar Styles** form as certain functions, such as Recurring Tasks, rely on these formats to display these special task bars in the Gantt Chart.

To hide a bar, type in the Legend an "*****" in front of the Name in the **Bar Styles** form. These bars will still be displayed in the Gantt Chart but will not be displayed in the Legend in Print Preview:

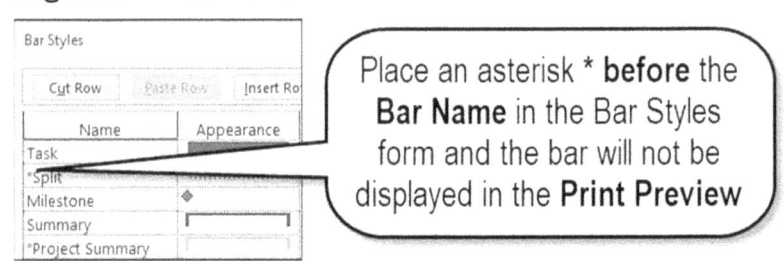

Place an asterisk * **before** the **Bar Name** in the Bar Styles form and the bar will not be displayed in the **Print Preview**

6.6 What has Happened to the Manual Page Breaks?

The **Manual page breaks** check box, which allowed printing and ignoring manual page breaks, in the **Print** form has been removed from Microsoft Project 2013 and 2016.

You will need to add the **Insert Page Break** Button on the **Quick Access** Toolbar to add manually-inserted breaks **Page Breaks**.

This button has been added to the Eastwood Harris Quick Access toolbar from **www.eh.com.au**, **Software & Downloads** page and import it from the **File**, **Options**, **Quick Access toolbar**, **Import/Export** command.

7 RESOURCE BASICS

7.1 How Many Resources Should I Have?

A resourced schedule may be created for the following purposes:

- ❖ **Estimating**. This type of schedule is used for estimating the cost and duration of a project or part of a project, such as a repeatable process. Many resources may be assigned to each task in an estimating schedule because it is not intended to status the schedule.

- ❖ **Control**. This type of schedule is used to monitor and control the progress of a project. In this situation the number of resources should be minimized as far as possible. This is because each resource assignment should be reviewed and possibly updated when the schedule is updated. Updating a large schedule, with many tasks and many resources assigned to each task becomes a very time consuming operation. In this situation the schedulers may lose sight of their primary aim of forecasting the project end date, resource requirement and possibly the Final Forecast Cost. The schedule is now in danger of becoming an expensive time recording system and thus unable to provide essential forecast information. Thus the number of resources in a control schedule should be limited to the maximum number required to satisfy control and reporting requirements.

7.2 The Balance Between the Number of Activities and Resources

On large or complex schedules, you need to maintain a balance between the number of activities and the number of resources that are to be planned and tracked. As a general rule, the more activities a schedule has, the fewer resources should be created and assigned to tasks.

When a schedule has a large number of tasks and a large number of resources assigned to each task, the scheduler may end up in a situation where project team members are unable to understand the schedule and the scheduler is unable to maintain the schedule.

You may consider in this situation using resources that represent skills or trades or crafts instead of individual people, and on very large projects using crews or teams.

Updating a project with resources is substantially harder than without resources. The software is hard enough to use without adding the complexity of lots of resources that may not add value to the schedule.

It is critical to enter the minimum number of resources into a schedule because they consume a substantial amount of time to update.

7.3 Durations and Assignments Change as Resources are Assigned

Microsoft Project has some complex user definable relationships that determine which parameters change when resources are added to tasks. For example, these relationships may result in durations or hours per resource reducing as resources are added to tasks.

This section will explain how resource assignments calculate and make some suggestions on how to set up the software, so the tasks calculate the way you expect.

7.3.1 Task Type – Fixed Duration, Fixed Units, Fixed Work

Users must understand the relationship between the following parameters:

- ❖ The task **Duration**,
- ❖ The **Work** (the number of hours required to complete a task), and
- ❖ The **Units per Time Period** (the rate of doing the work or number of people working on the task).

The relationship is:

Duration x Units per Time Period = Work

For example, a 2-day task at 8 hours per day has a **Duration** of 2 x 8 =16 hours. If 2 people are assigned to the task the **Units per Time Period** is 2.00 or 200% and the work is 16 x 2 = 32 hours.

There are three **Default task type:** options and the default is assigned in the **File, Options, Schedule** tab. Each new task is set with this Task Type. It may be changed at any time for each task in the **Task Type** field which may be accessed in a number of places such as the **Task Type** column in the **Task** form, **Task Details** form and the **Task Information** form.

The **Default task type** decides how this relationship operates when one parameter changes. They are:

Fixed Duration — The **Duration** stays constant when either the **Units per Time Period** or **Work** are changed.

A change to the **Duration** changes the **Work**.

Fixed Units — The **Units per Time Period** stay constant when either the **Duration** or **Work** is changed.

A change to the **Units per Time Period** changes the **Duration**.

Note: This is the authors preferred default.

Fixed Work — The **Work** stays constant if either **Duration** or **Units per Time Period** are changed.

A change to the **Work** changes the **Duration**.

Therefore, your estimate will not change when you change **Duration** or **Units per Time Period**.

7.3.2 Effort driven or Non Effort driven?

The **Task Effort** is the sum of the Work (hours) of all Work Type resources assigned to a task. The **Effort driven** option determines how the effort is calculated as resources are added or removed from a **Fixed Units** or **Fixed Duration** task. There are two options:

Effort driven — When a resource is added or removed from a task, the **Task Effort** assigned to a task remains constant. Therefore, the Work of existing Resources is reduced when a new resource is assigned. Adding or removing resources from a task will leave the total effort assigned to a task constant unless all resources are removed or a change is made to the work of existing resource assignments.

Non Effort driven — When a resource is added to or removed from a task, the **Resource Effort** or **Work** of other resources remains constant. Adding or deleting resources increases or decreases the total task effort and will not change the effort of assigned recourses.

Note: This is the authors preferred default.

In summary, as you assign resources:

- ❖ If you want the total number of hours assigned to stay constant, then make the task **Effort** driven.
- ❖ If you wish to assign each resource with its own hours or units per time period, then make the task **Non Effort** driven.

Note: A **Fixed Work** task is automatically **Effort driven**.

7.3.3 Task Type and Effort driven Options

If you are not sure which option to use then it is recommended that **Non Effort driven** be used as a default. This option prevents changes to Task Durations and/or existing Resource assignments, as Resources are added or removed from a task.

- ❖ Select **Fixed Units** for activities when the Units per time period must stay constant as either the Duration or Work is changed. For example, a crew of 1 Excavator and 3 Trucks must stay constant as the Duration or Work is changed.
- ❖ Select **Fixed Duration** for activities when the duration must not change as either resource Units per time period or Work is changed.
- ❖ Select **Fixed Work** if you wish the Work to stay constant as the duration is changed. The Task will be made **Effort driven** automatically with the **Effort driven** option grayed out. For example, a programmer assigned full-time for a week will have 40 hours' work. When the duration is doubled to 2 weeks, the programmer will work 50% of the time over 2 weeks but still work 40 hours. If you assign another person to help then the total Work will remain at 40 hours and the Duration not change.

The default for new Tasks is set in the **File**, **Options**, **Schedule** tab, **Scheduling options for this project:**, select [All New Projects] from the drop down box and all new projects will have these as their default options.

7.4 Assigning Resources to Tasks

There are many methods to assign resources to tasks. In summary, they are:

- ❖ Highlight one or more tasks that you want to assign resources. Click the **Assign Resources** icon on the **Resources** toolbar to display the **Assign Resources** form.

- ❖ Open the bottom window and display the **Task Details Form** or **Task Form** or **Task Name Form**, then select the **Resource Work** or **Resource Cost** option from the **Format, Details** option or by right-clicking in the form.

- ❖ Double-click on a **Task** name or click on the **Task Information** icon to open the **Task Information** form and select the **Resources** tab.

- ❖ Display the **Resource Names** column and type in the resource assignment.

7.5 Resources and Summary Tasks

- ❖ Summary tasks may be assigned **Fixed Costs** and **Resources**.

- ❖ A summary task is set to **Fixed Duration** and **Non Effort- Driven**. This setting may not be changed. An increase in duration will increase Work and the **Resource Units** will stay constant.

- ❖ It is recommended that unless a Summary task Work resource assignment and costs are required to vary in proportion to the Summary task duration, then Work resources should not be assigned to a Summary task. You should consider using Fixed Costs, Cost resource or a Material resource if appropriate.

8 UPDATING ESSENTIALS

8.1 Baselines and Updating a Project

After a schedule has been reviewed and approved, it should be baselined before it is updated for the first time. Setting the Baseline copies the **Early Start** and **Early Finish**, the **Original Duration** and each resource's **Costs** and **Work** into Baseline fields.

A Microsoft Project Baseline is not a complete baseline because it does not record Constraints, Relationships, Float or the Critical Path.

Once the Baseline is set you will be able to update your plan and compare the progress with the original plan and be able to see:

If the planned progress has been achieved,

If the project is ahead or behind schedule, and

By how much in time and cost.

A Baseline is set by selecting **Project**, **Schedule** group, **Set Baseline**.

There are a number of options and forms available to update project tasks after setting the Baseline.

Irrespective of which forms are used, there are two main methods to update a project:

- ❖ Auto Status the schedule by allowing the software to automatically update the tasks, as if the project progressed exactly according to schedule. Then, if required, adjust tasks to reflect actual events and revisions, or
- ❖ Update each task one by one.

8.2 Which Baseline Should Be Used?

After a project has progressed it may be necessary to set a new Baseline.

This may occur when the scope of a project has changed and a new baseline is required to measure progress against, but at the same time you may also want to keep a copy of the original baseline.

A new Baseline may be used to display the effect of scope changes on a plan by setting a Baseline, adding the scope change and comparing the revised schedule with the Baseline.

The **Baseline** data may be reviewed in some Views such as the **Task Details Form**, in columns and on the Bar Chart. You will be able to display the **Baseline 1** to **10** and **Interim Plan** dates and durations in columns and as bars on the Gantt Chart but not in the forms. **Baseline 1** to **10** also do not have variance columns.

Therefore, it is recommended that the current baseline be saved as the **Baseline** since the data is more accessible from the **Baseline** than **Baseline 1** to **10**. Previous baselines should be copied to **Baselines 1** to **10** and preserved as a record.

Another benefit of using **Baseline** is that it has **Variance Start**, **Variance Finish** and **Variance Duration** columns that are not available with other Baselines, but may be calculated using a Calculated Field.

Note: The downside of using one of the Baselines 1 to 10 is that it is not possible to easily identify what the Baseline was set for as there is no inbuilt way of naming these baselines. One option is the record notes on the baselines in the **Advanced Properties** form, **Comments:** section.

8.3 Principles of Updating a Program

Ideally, scheduling software has one current **Data Date** and the function of it is to:

- Separate the completed parts of tasks from incomplete parts of tasks,
- Calculate or record all costs and hours to date before the **Data Date**, and to forecast costs and hours to go after the **Data Date**,
- Calculate the **Finish Date** of an in-progress task from the **Data Date** plus the **Remaining Duration** over the **Task Calendar**.

Therefore, in a properly updated Microsoft Project program, the **Status Date** should be used as the **Data Date** and not the Microsoft Project **Current Date** field because the **Current Date** field changes to today's date each time a file is opened:

- **Completed** tasks would have Actual Start and Actual Finish Dates in the past.
- **In progress** tasks would have the Actual Start and Actual Duration in the past, and the Early Finish and Remaining Duration in the Future.
- **Unstarted** tasks should be in the future.

Note: In Microsoft Project it is relatively simple to be in a situation where you have complete or in-progress tasks with start dates later than the **Status Date**, and/or incomplete or un-started tasks with a finish date earlier than the **Status Date**. This is an unrealistic situation, which is more difficult to achieve in other scheduling software packages. Care should be taken to avoid this situation and checks made after the schedule has been updated.

Note: The Eastwood Harris template found at the **www.eh.com.au** website **Software & Downloads** page has a **Tracking Table** with an additional column showing what is required to do to ensure the tasks are correctly updated. This is created in Text 30 as a Calculated Field.

8.4 In-progress Task Finish Date Calculation

Many planning and scheduling packages calculate a task Finish Date from the Data Date plus the Remaining Duration over the Task or Resource Calendar, whichever is applicable.

Unlike most planning and scheduling software packages, Microsoft Project ignores the **Current Date** and **Status Date** when calculating an in-progress task. It calculates a task **Finish Date** from the **Actual Start Date** plus the **Duration** and effectively ignores the **Remaining Duration** for normal progress calculation.

There is an in-built proportional link between **Duration**, **% Complete, Actual Duration** and **Remaining Duration**. It is not possible to unlink these fields (as in other scheduling software) and therefore not possible to enter the **Remaining Duration** independently of the **% Complete**.

Dur	% Comp.	Act. Dur.	Rem. Dur.	August 11 M T W T F S S	August 18 M T W T F S S	August 25 M T W T F
10d	0%	0d	10d			
10d	25%	2.5d	7.5d			
10d	100%	10d	0d			

Thus **% Complete** field is the **% Duration** of a task.

8.5 Understanding the % Completes

Microsoft Project has three inbuilt % completes:

- ❖ **% Complete** – This is the **Duration % Complete**.
  - ➢ In **Detailed** Tasks the **Duration, Actual Duration, Remaining Duration** and **% Complete** are linked and may not be unlinked,
  - ➢ The **% Complete** is calculated by dividing the **Actual Duration** by the **Duration**.
  - ➢ In **Summary Tasks** it is calculated by the sum of the **Detailed Tasks Actual Durations** and dividing by the sum of the **Detailed Tasks Durations**.
  - ➢ A **Milestone** assigned a 100% Complete will not always contribute to the Summary % Complete:

#	Task Name	Dur	% Complete
1	▲ Summary	5d	0%
2	A	0d	100%
3	B	5d	0%
4	C	0d	0%
5			
6	▲ Summary	5d	99%
7	A	0d	100%
8	B	5d	100%
9	C	0d	0%

- ❖ % Work – This represents the amount of work completed:
  - ➢ The **Work, Actual Work, Remaining Work, Work** and **% Work** are linked and may not be unlinked,
  - ➢ The **% Work** is calculated by dividing the **Actual Work** by the **Work**.
  - ➢ The **% Work** and **% Complete** are normally linked, thus a change in the **% Complete** will change the **% Work**. Thus, the Actual Work is updated automatically.

- The **% Work** and **% Complete** are unlinked in the **Updating task status updates resource status** option in the **File**, **Options**, **Schedule** tab. When this is unchecked, then the **Actual Work** and **Remaining Work** may be edited separately from the **Actual Durations** and **Remaining Durations**. This should be unchecked if you wish to enter the actual work from timesheets etc.

❖ **Physical % Complete** – It is useful in the situation when the % complete of completed work is required to be displayed, based on completed deliverables and not durations or labor hours.
  - This is independent of durations and work.
  - It is not summarized against summary tasks.
  - It may be displayed by creating a bar as per below:

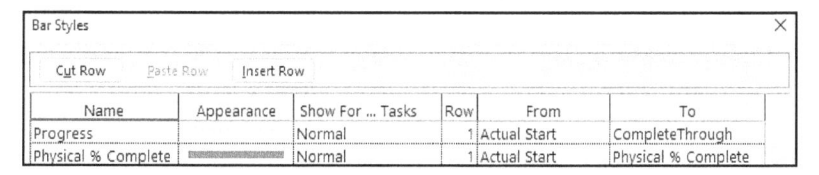

Name	Appearance	Show For ... Tasks	Row	From	To
Progress		Normal	1	Actual Start	CompleteThrough
Physical % Complete		Normal	1	Actual Start	Physical % Complete

8.6 Current Date and Status Date

Microsoft Project has two project data date fields that may be displayed as vertical lines on the schedule. These dates may be edited from the **Project**, **Properties**, **Project Information** form:

- ❖ **Current Date** – This date is set to the computer's date each time a project file is opened. It is used for calculating **Earned Value** data when a **Status Date** has not been set. The time of the **Current Date** is set by default to the start time of a day, see the picture below.

- ❖ **Status Date** – This field is blank by default with a value of **NA**. The Status Date will not change when the project is saved and reopened at a later date. It overrides the **Current Date** for calculating **Earned Value** data and is set by default to the finish time of a day, see the picture below.

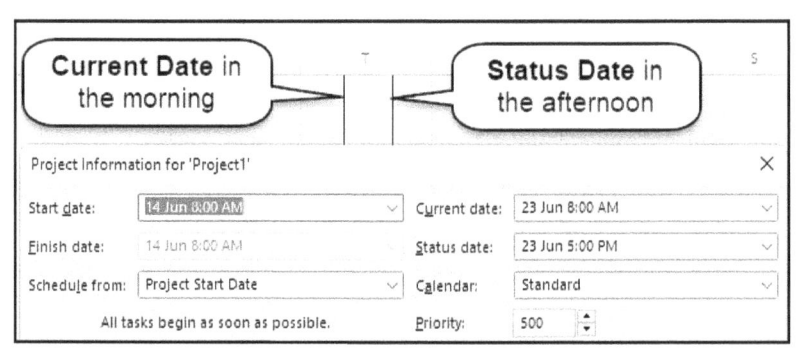

Current Date in the morning

Status Date in the afternoon

Project Information for 'Project1'				
Start date:	14 Jun 8:00 AM	Current date:	23 Jun 8:00 AM	
Finish date:	14 Jun 8:00 AM	Status date:	23 Jun 5:00 PM	
Schedule from:	Project Start Date	Calendar:	Standard	
	All tasks begin as soon as possible.	Priority:	500	

Note: It is recommended that the **Status Date** is set and displayed as a vertical line on a progressed schedule and the **Current Date** not displayed, because the **Current Date** represents the date today and does not normally represent any scheduling significance. It is unfortunate that the default Microsoft Project Views do not display the **Status Date** in the Gantt chart.

8.7 Auto Updating Using Update Project

The Microsoft Project facility titled **Update Progress** is used for updating a project as if it had progressed according to plan. This function sets **Actual Start** and **Actual Finish** dates, % **Complete** and **Remaining Durations** in proportion to a user-assigned date, and also sets the **Status Date**.

Select **Project**, **Update Project** located in the **Status** group to open the **Update Project** form:

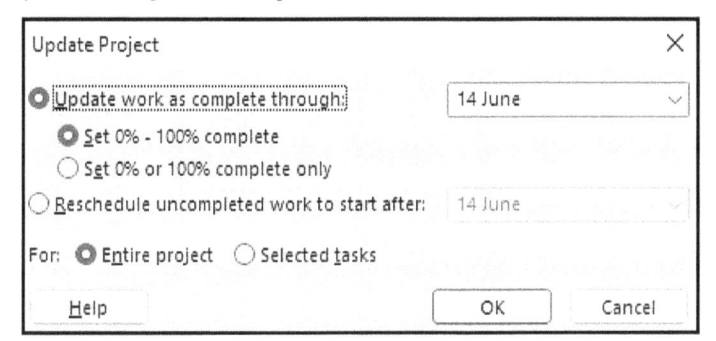

```
Update Project                                              ×

● Update work as complete through:        14 June        ⌄
   ● Set 0% - 100% complete
   ○ Set 0% or 100% complete only
○ Reschedule uncompleted work to start after:  14 June   ⌄

For:  ● Entire project   ○ Selected tasks

   Help                                    OK      Cancel
```

There are two options under **Update work as complete through:** which apply to in-progress tasks only.

❖ **Set 0% – 100 % complete** and this is the recommended option which sets the progress in line with the **Status Date**, or

❖ **Set 0% or 100 % complete only.** This option leaves the % Complete at zero until the task is 100% complete. This option supports the progress measurement philosophy of not awarding progress until the task is complete, but tasks often look behind schedule and the Actual and Remaining Durations are calculated incorrectly.

8.8 Moving Incomplete Work into the Future by Splitting

There is a feature which will schedule the **Incomplete Work** of an **In-Progress** task to start on a specific date in the future:

- ❖ If you want to apply this operation to some tasks, then these tasks should be selected first.
- ❖ Select the **File, Options, Schedule** tab and ensure the **Split in-progress tasks** option is checked otherwise this function will not operate.
- ❖ Select **Project**, **Update Project** located in the **Status** group to open the **Update Project** form:

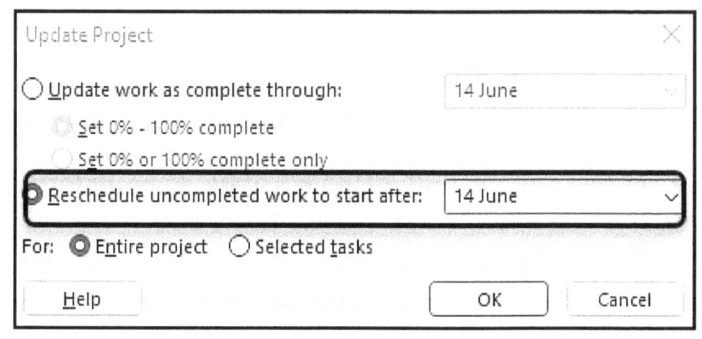

[Update Project form showing: Update work as complete through: 14 June; Set 0% - 100% complete; Set 0% or 100% complete only; Reschedule uncompleted work to start after: 14 June (selected); For: Entire project / Selected tasks; Help, OK, Cancel buttons]

- ❖ Click on the **Reschedule uncompleted work to start after:** radio button.
- ❖ Specify the date after which incomplete work should commence in the drop-down box to the right and click on the OK button.

Note: This function does not set the **Status Date** and may be different to the **Status Date**. It is therefore effectively another **Data Date**.

8.9 Where is the Tracking Toolbar?

Microsoft Project 365, 2021, 2019, 2016 and 2013 do not have a dedicated **Tracking** toolbar as in earlier version and some tracking commands can be found in the **Task**, **Schedule** group and **Project**, **Status** tab.

To create a complete **Tracking** toolbar; go to **File**, **Options**, **Customize Ribbon**, click on [New Tab], click on [Rename...] and name both the tab and the group **Tracking.** Now select and add the commands listed on the left side of the pane to the newly created **Tracking** toolbar.

Alternatively, you may add the missing buttons to the existing toolbars.

You may find the following commands very useful and should be added to your Quick Access Toolbar:

- ❖ **Mark on Track** updates the selected task as if it has proceeded exactly as it was scheduled. An in-progress or completed task could be dragged to where it actually happened and then the button clicked to progress the task.

- ❖ **Reschedule Work** will split a task that is behind schedule and place the incomplete portion after the Status Date. For this function to work the check the **Split in Progress task** box in the **File**, **Options**, **Schedule** tab, **Split in-progress tasks** must be checked.

The following commands you may also find useful:

- **Progress Line** will add a progress line that shows if tasks are ahead or behind schedule. Right click on the **Gantt Chart** to open the menu and select **Progress Lines** to open the **Progress Lines** form where the lines are formatted. A Baseline should be set to provide a comparison to the original plan. Multiple Progress lines may be recorded.

- **Percent Complete** buttons set the percent complete as indicated by the button and may be used in conjunction with the Reschedule Work button.
  Note: The use of the 25%, 50% and 75% buttons will usually result in an incorrectly updated schedule with complete work in the future or incomplete work in the past and should be used with caution.

- **Update Tasks** opens the **Update Tasks** form where you may update individual tasks.

- **Update Project** opens the **Update Project** form where you may update a complete project to a new **Status Date** as if it went according to plan.

- Displays the **Project Statistics** form.

8.10 Why Do Calculation Options – Move end of completed parts Not Work?

These new functions, introduced in Microsoft Project 2002, were intended to assist schedulers to place the new tasks as they are added to the schedule in a logical position with respect to the **Status Date**. This function is difficult to use and some practice is required to make it work properly and you should consider **NOT** using it.

Here are some tips if you are unable to get it to work:

- ❖ These options are activated from the **File**, **Options**, **Schedule** tab, under the **Scheduling** options for this project: 'Project Name':
- ❖ If the **Status Date** has not been set then the Current Date is used, and this is often an irrelevant date, so ensure you set the **Status Date**.
- ❖ For all these options to operate all four of the following parameters must be met:
  - ➢ The **Split in-progress tasks option** in the **File**, **Options**, **Schedule** tab must be checked, and
  - ➢ The required option on the **Schedule** tab must be checked before the task is added or edited, and
  - ➢ The **Updating task status updates resource status option** on the Calculation options for this project: section must be checked, and
  - ➢ The Task **MUST NOT BE** assigned **Task Duration Type** of **Fixed Duration**.
- ❖ These options may **NOT** be turned on and off to recalculate all tasks. The options only work on new tasks when they are added to a schedule or when a task is updated by changing the % Complete.
- ❖ This function will ignore constraints, even when the **Schedule Option Tasks will always honor their constraint dates** has been set.

- ❖ This function may not be applied to existing schedules, but only to new tasks if the options are set before the tasks are added, or when a task % Complete is updated.

This function has some restrictions:

- ❖ Existing schedules may not be opened and the function applied.
- ❖ When the **Move start of remaining parts before status date forward to status date** is used, it will change any **Actual Start** date that you have entered prior to entering a % Complete. Changing an Actual Date is not a desirable event.

Notes:

- ❖ This option should be used with caution and users should ensure they fully understand how this function operates by updating a simple practice schedule multiple times.
- ❖ It is recommended that this function should not be used and tasks updated manually, as it is very difficult to perfect the use of these functions and it is simple to make undesirable changes to Actual Data.

8.11 Comparing Progress with Baseline

There will normally be changes to the schedule dates and more often than not these are delays. The full extent of the changes may not be apparent without a Baseline bar to compare with the updated schedule.

To display the **Baseline Bar** in the **Bar Chart** either use:

- ❖ The **Gantt Chart Format**, **Bar Styles** function, or
- ❖ Manually create a Baseline Bar, or
- ❖ Create a View with the Baseline bar displayed.
- ❖ You may use the **Gantt Chart Wizard**, but this should only be used with projects created with schedules created with Microsoft Project 2007 and earlier due to the incompatibility of the formatting options between 2007 and earlier versions and 2010 and later versions; resulting in some bars being hidden.
- ❖ You will need to add the add **Gantt Chart Wizard** button to the **Quick Access Toolbar** to use it.

8.12 Progress Lines

Some users like to display **Progress Lines**, which are usually shown as zigzag lines on the Gantt Chart, showing how far ahead or behind the project tasks are.

Select **Gantt Chart Format**, **Gridlines**, and select **Progress Lines** from the dropdown to open the **Progress line** form where the progress lines may be formatted:

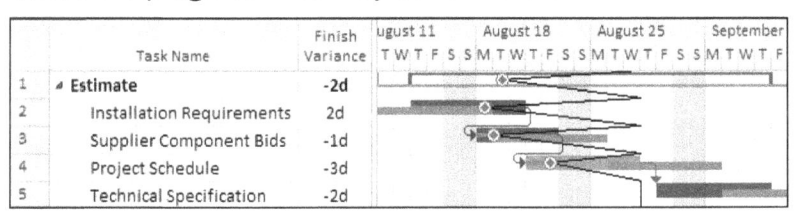

	Task Name	Finish Variance
1	⊿ Estimate	-2d
2	Installation Requirements	2d
3	Supplier Component Bids	-1d
4	Project Schedule	-3d
5	Technical Specification	-2d

8.13 Simple Procedure for Updating a Schedule – Using Auto Status

The following process should be considered for people who require one simple method of updating a schedule. This may not suit all situations especially when a project is way off plan:

- Set the Baseline by selecting **Project**, **Schedule**, **Set Baseline**.
- Display the Baseline bars by selecting **Gantt Chart Format**, **Bar Styles** function and select the newly created baseline.
- Display the **Status Date** gridline, select **Gantt Chart Format**, **Format**, **Gridlines**, select **Status Date**.
- Select **Project**, **Status**, **Update Project** to open the **Update Project** form and select **Set 0% – 100 % Complete**, set the date in the form to the new **Status Date**,
- The project will be updated as if it has progressed exactly as planned and the **Status Date** should now be displayed in the bar chart.
- Displaying the **Tracking Table** may assist here. **Note:** The Eastwood Harris template found at the **www.eh.com.au** website **Software & Downloads** page has a **Tracking Table** with an additional column showing what is required to do to ensure the tasks are correctly updated.

- ❖ Now adjust the task dates by dragging the bars or entering the dates in the appropriate column; the order that the actions take place is important:
  - ➢ **Complete tasks** should have the Actual Start and then the Actual Finish dates adjusted, in this order, to match the dates that the task actually started and actually finished. If you adjust the Finish date first then the Start date, you will then have to readjust the Finish date again.
  - ➢ **Completed Milestones** will be changed to a Task when an Actual Finish date is entered, so ensure you only enter an Actual Start and 100% if a Milestone is complete, **DO NOT ENTER AN ACTUAL FINISH**,
  - ➢ **In-Progress tasks** should have the Actual Start entered first, then the task bar dragged or Duration adjusted so the finish date is where it is expected to finish, and finally the **% Complete** and/or **Actual Duration** adjusted so the progress is at the **Status Date**. The 🗒 **Mark on Track** is useful here as updates the selected task as if it has proceeded exactly as it was scheduled.
  - ➢ **Unstarted tasks** should have their logic and durations revised.
- ❖ Add any scope changes to the schedule.
- ❖ Save the project with a new filename and save for future reference.

8.14 Procedure for Detailed Updating

This procedure is suited to people who wish to update a schedule properly and make sure the Actual dates and Remaining Durations of each Task are correct. It has small but important differences to the previous process:

- ❖ Ensure that everyone on the project team is aware of the reporting cycle, the updating procedure and review process.
- ❖ Collect accurate and complete status information.
- ❖ Set the Baseline by selecting **Project**, **Schedule**, **Set Baseline**.
- ❖ Display the Baseline bars by selecting **Gantt Chart Format**, **Format**, **Baseline** and select the newly created baseline.
- ❖ Select the **Gantt Chart** view and you may find the Tracking Table useful to apply.
- ❖ Display the Variance columns as required; the **Finish Variance** is always a popular column to display.
- ❖ Display the **Status Date** gridline, select **Gantt Chart Format**, **Format**, **Gridlines**, and select **Status Date**.
- ❖ Now enter the task status for each task one at a time by entering the information in the appropriate column.
- ❖ The order in which the actions take place is important:
  - ➢ **Complete tasks** should have the Actual Start and then the Actual Finish dates adjusted, in this order, to the date that the task actually started and actually finished. If you adjust the Finish date first, then the Start date, you will have to readjust the Finish date again.

- ➢ **Completed Milestones** will be changed to a Task if an Actual Finish date is entered, so only enter an Actual Start and 100% when a Milestone is complete, **DO NOT ENTER AN ACTUAL FINISH**,
- ➢ **In-Progress tasks** should have the Actual Start entered first, then the task bar dragged or Duration adjusted so the Finish Date is where it is estimated to finish and finally the **% Complete** and/or **Actual Duration** adjusted so the progress is at the **Status Date.** This may be adjusted with the **Mark on Track** button as this function updates the selected task as if it has proceeded exactly as it was scheduled.
- ➢ Tasks that are behind schedule may be split with the **Reschedule Work** icon on the **Tracking** toolbar. Make sure that the **File**, **Options**, **Schedule** tab, **Split in-progress tasks** box is checked:

Task Name	% Comp.	August 11	August 18	August 25	Septe
Before Splitting	20%				
After Splitting	20%				

- ➢ **Unstarted tasks** should have their logic and durations revised.
- ❖ Add any scope changes to the schedule.
- ❖ Save the project with a new filename.

8.15 Preparing to Update with Resources

Updating Microsoft Project schedules with resources:

- ❖ Uses a number of features that are very interactive and difficult to comprehend,
- ❖ Requires experience in the software,
- ❖ Needs significant time to complete the process, and
- ❖ As a result, it is often difficult to achieve the desired outcome.

It is suggested that before you work on a live project, that you:

- ❖ Create a simple schedule with a couple of tasks and assign two or three resources against each task,
- ❖ Set the **Options** to reflect the way you want to enter the information and how you want Microsoft Project to calculate, and
- ❖ Go through the updating process with dummy data and then check that the results are as you expected.

You will need to consider how the measure of progress at the summary task level will be displayed:

❖ The **% Complete** is the **% Duration Complete** and the **Summary Task % Complete** is based on the proportion of all the Details Tasks Actual Durations divided by the sum of all the Details Tasks Durations. The summary % Complete may often be very misleading. The picture below shows the project is 20% through the duration, but the % Complete shows 60%:

	Task Name	% Comp.	4	11	18	25	Sep 1	8
1	⊿ Summary	60%						
2	Task 1	100%						
3	Task 2	100%						
4	Task 3	100%						
5	Task 4	100%						
6	Task 5	100%						
7	Task 6	20%						

❖ The **% Work** field is calculated from the proportion of the **Actual Work** to **Work** and is summarized at summary task correctly:

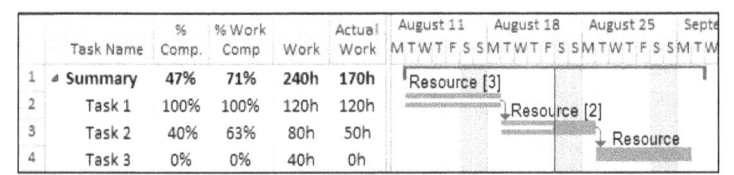

	Task Name	% Comp.	% Work Comp	Work	Actual Work	August 11	August 18	August 25	Septe
1	⊿ Summary	47%	71%	240h	170h	Resource [3]			
2	Task 1	100%	100%	120h	120h		Resource [2]		
3	Task 2	40%	63%	80h	50h			Resource	
4	Task 3	0%	0%	40h	0h				

❖ The **% Work** and **% Complete** fields may be unlinked with the **File, Option, Calculation** options for this project: tab **Updating task status updates resource status:** option. If unlinked, the **% Work** may be different from **% Complete**. See the picture above. This allows the editing of **Resource Work** without the **% Complete** being changed with some options.

Other points to consider are:

❖ Do you wish Microsoft Project to calculate the resource **Actual Costs** with the option **File**, **Option**, **Calculation options for this project:**, **Actual costs are always calculated by Microsoft Project** checked?

❖ Do you wish your incomplete tasks to be split and scheduled to start after a date using **Project**, **Status** group, **Update Project** button, and check **Reschedule uncompleted tasks to start after:** radio button in conjunction with the **Split** task option?

❖ Microsoft Project 365, 2021, 2019, 2016 and 2013 calculates differently to earlier versions when the option **Actual costs are always calculated by Project** are unchecked when the activity is at 100%.

❖ In earlier versions the **Actual Cost** was unchanged but could be manually changed from that point on.

❖ In Microsoft Project 365, 2021, 2019, 2016 and 2013 the software changes the **Actual Costs** to zero when unchecked, which would normally be less desirable, and the **Actual Costs** must then be manually entered.

8.16　Updating Resources

There are a number of places that resources may be updated:

- ❖ The **Task Details** form, **Task Information** form, **Task** form, **Resource** form, **Resource Name** form may be used to enter the quantities and costs to date and quantities to complete. Using this method, it is simple to end up with actual work and costs in the future or remaining work and cost in the past, which is illogical and should be avoided.

- ❖ The **Task Usage View** and **Resource Usage View** may be used to enter the data per day or week depending on the timescale. This method takes more effort but will ensure Actuals are in the past and Remaining Work and Costs are in the future.

A couple of other points:

- ❖ **Fixed Costs** updates automatically in proportion to the **% Complete**. **Cost Resources** do not have a Quantity, allows a little more flexibility than Fixed Costs.

- ❖ When **Actual costs are always calculated by Project** is unchecked Actual Costs are **NOT** calculated when task progress is assigned and you will need to enter your own **Actual Costs**. This option also applies to **Fixed Costs** which may result in the **Fixed Cost** and **Total Cost** having a different value, whereas with resources the **Cost** always equals the **Actual Cost** plus **Remaining Costs**.

- ❖ **Cost to Complete** are **ALWAYS** calculated by Microsoft Project from the Resource Rates.

- ❖ If you assign Overtime to a resource, make sure you have an Overtime rate; otherwise, as you assign Overtime the Forecast Cost will reduce.

9 CREATING NEW PROJECTSS

9.1 Standardizing Projects

It is often important to be able to create new schedules that have standard characteristics, such as calendars tailored with your local or organization's holidays, or layouts and filters to present schedules in a standard format. There are several methods of standardizing new projects:

- **Global.mpt** which is used to create new projects when the **File**, **New**, **Blank Project** option is used,
- Creating and saving a **Templates**,
- Creating a "Standard Project" and copying it.

9.2 Global.mpt

The **Global.mpt** function may be used to standardize projects, only if you are the only person creating new projects.

- A new blank project copies default values such as the Standard Calendar from the **Global.mpt** file.
- The **Global.mpt** file may be edited using the **File**, **Info**, **Organize** utility. The source project has to be open to copy data into the Global.mpt.
- The **Global.mpt** may not be opened with Microsoft Project and is part of the Microsoft Project Installation on each computer.

Note: The author has found a number of issues with the **Global.mpt** file shipped with a standard load of Microsoft Project 365, 2021, 2019, 2016 and 2013 and recommends using an edited **Personal Template**.

9.3 Microsoft Project Template Changes

Microsoft Project 365, 2021, 2019, 2016 and 2013 templates operate differently to earlier versions of Microsoft Project and there are some important changes that need to be understood by users of earlier versions of Microsoft Project.

- **Templates** that are saved on your computer are now titled **Personal Templates** in Microsoft Project 365, 2021, 2019, 2016 and 2013,
- A default location for your personal templates needs to be created and your software mapped to this location before the **Personal Templates** function will operate:

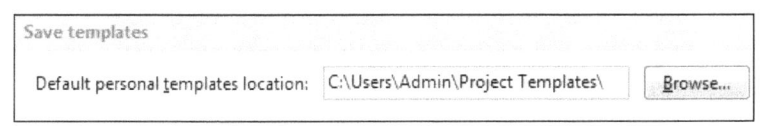

```
Save templates
Default personal templates location:  C:\Users\Admin\Project Templates\    Browse...
```

- Select **File**, **Options**, **Save** and set your **Default personal templates location:** here,
- At this point in time **Personal Templates** may now be saved and used to create projects.

Note: To use **Personal Templates** you **MUST** set your Personal directory in **File**, **Options**, **Save**.

9.4 Understanding Templates

A template is a complete project that is saved and then copied in the process of creating a new project.

- ***.mpt** file format is used for saving Microsoft Project **Personal Templates**.
- The default location for **Personal Templates** is set in the **File**, **Options**, **Save** tab, **Save templates** section.

- Select **File**, **New** to open the start-up **Task Pane**. There are several options for template locations:
  - **FEATURED**, this provides a number of sample templates and the ability to search for available online templates.
  - **PERSONAL**, this will allow you to open templates on your computer. As mentioned earlier, a Template directory must be specified first for this option to become available.
- Organizational templates may be accessed by:
  - Allowing people to copy the organizational templates from a corporate location, or receive them by email, and save them on the local drive. This process is suitable when the users do not always have a network connection.
  - Mapping the **User templates** directory to a location on a corporate network drive.

9.5   Eastwood Harris Template

A Microsoft Project template in ***.mpp** format may be downloaded from the Eastwood Harris web site at from the **www.eh.com.au**, **Software & Downloads** page that has a number of the issues with Microsoft Project defaults and other setting resolved. The changes to the Global.mpt default settings are listed on the web site.

You may wish to download this file, open it and save it as a **Personal Template** and use this file instead of the **Blank Project** option as it has some formatting issues resolved.

9.6 Copying Views, Tables and Filters

As part of creating a Template or working on a project you may wish to bring in **Views, Tables or Filters** from an existing project.

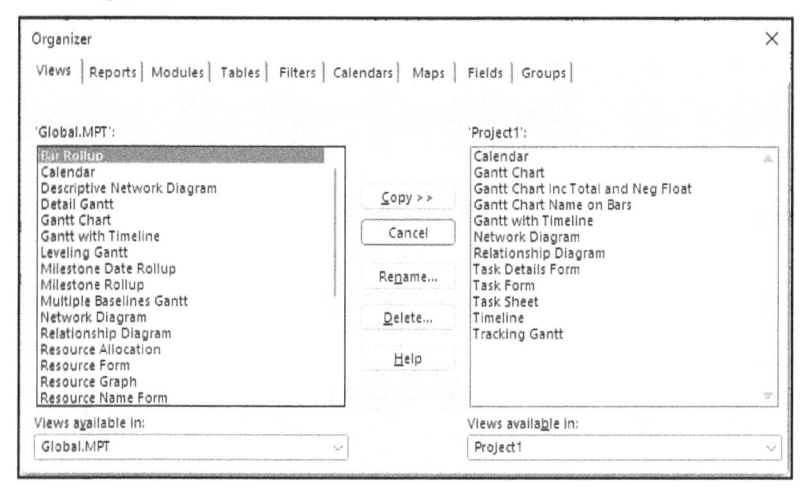

The **Organizer** function is used to copy information between projects or to update the **Global.mpt**.

❖ Select **File, Info, Organizer** to open the **Organizer** form.
❖ The projects you want to copy settings to and from will have to be opened in order to copy data from one schedule to another, except for the **Global.mpt** project.
❖ The **Organizer** function is used for renaming and deleting most items such as **Tables**, **Views** and **Calendars**.
❖ The two tabs with titles that are not self-explanatory are:
  ➢ **Maps** – These are predefined tables for exporting data, and
  ➢ **Modules** – These are Visual Basic Macros.

10 OTHER THINGS OF INTEREST

10.1 Editing Tool Bars

It is recommended you customize your menus by:

- Firstly, to allow more buttons to be displayed on the **Quick Access Toolbar**, right click on the Toolbar and select **Show Quick Access Toolbar Below the Ribbon** to move the Quick Access Toolbar below the Ribbon Toolbar.
- Secondly, it is recommended that you hide the Ribbon Toolbar by Right-clicking on the Ribbon Toolbar and display the Ribbon Toolbar Menu. Then click on **Collapse the Ribbon** to hide the Ribbon Toolbar. When you click in the Gantt Chart area the Ribbon will minimize and more work area will be available allowing you to see more tasks.
- Thirdly, it is recommended that you download the **Microsoft Project Quick Access Toolbar** from the www.eh.com.au website **Software & Downloads** page, unzip it by double clicking on the file and dragging it to your Desktop. Then import the toolbar using **File**, **Options**, **Quick Access Toolbar**, **Import/Export**. This has all the commonly used commands on the Quick Access Toolbar.

To do further editing to the Tool bar icons:

- **Right-Click** in the toolbar area,
- Select **Customize the Ribbon…**,
- Select the **All Commands** option,
- Drag icons onto the required tool bar, or
- Drag icons off the toolbar to remove them.

10.2 Dynamically Linking Cells

It is also possible to dynamically link data to other programs such as an Excel spreadsheet:

Copy the data from the spreadsheet,

- ❖ Select the cell position in the table where the data is to be pasted in Microsoft Project,
- ❖ Select **Paste Special** and then select the **Paste Link** and **Text Data** options,
- ❖ The data will be pasted into the cell(s) and changes to linked cells in the spreadsheet or other program will be reflected in Microsoft Project.
- ❖ The linked cell will have a little triangle in the bottom right-hand side: 8 May
- ❖ Be careful when linking date fields as this may set an unwanted constraint.
- ❖ When you reopen the project schedule at a later date you will be asked if you wish to refresh the data from the other application.
- ❖ Delete or change the cell data to remove a link.
- ❖ Double-click on the little triangle in the bottom right hand side of the cell to open the link.
- ❖ It is also possible to link one or more cells in a schedule with another cell in the same schedule, so a change in one cell will change all the other linked cell(s). Again use the **Paste Link** option.

10.3 How Does Negative Float Calculate for Summary Activities?

The lowest value of the Total Float of incomplete tasks is adopted by the summary task, Sub Task 1 in the picture below and has adopted 3 days:

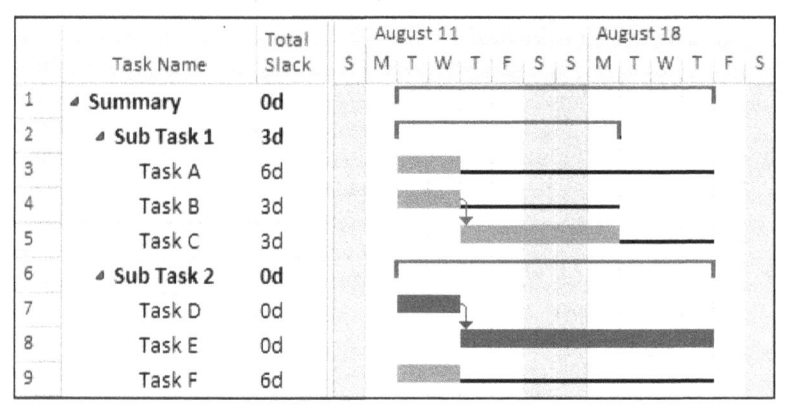

#	Task Name	Total Slack
1	▲ Summary	0d
2	▲ Sub Task 1	3d
3	Task A	6d
4	Task B	3d
5	Task C	3d
6	▲ Sub Task 2	0d
7	Task D	0d
8	Task E	0d
9	Task F	6d

In the picture below, Task C is the latest task under Sub Task 1 and has Float, but Sub Task 1 has adopted zero float from Task D the lowest float value.

#	Task Name	Total Slack
1	▲ Summary	0d
2	▲ Sub Task 1	0d
3	Task A	6d
4	Task B	3d
5	Task C	3d
6	Task D	0d
7	▲ Sub Task 2	0d
8	Task E	0d
9	Task F	6d

Now the project has progressed and the task with zero float is complete. Sub Task 1 has 3 days' Float:

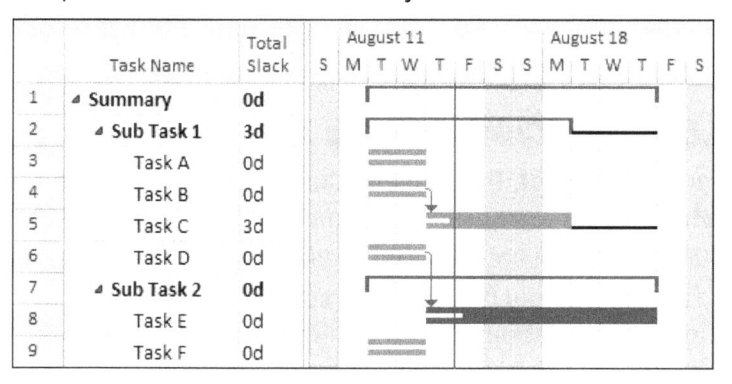

#	Task Name	Total Slack
1	⊿ Summary	0d
2	⊿ Sub Task 1	3d
3	Task A	0d
4	Task B	0d
5	Task C	3d
6	Task D	0d
7	⊿ Sub Task 2	0d
8	Task E	0d
9	Task F	0d

10.4 Float and Constraints

The following principles apply to constraints:

❖ **Early** constraints operate on **Early dates**,
❖ **Late** constraints operate on **Late dates**,
❖ **Start** constraints operate on **Start dates**, and
❖ **Finish** constraints operate on **Finish dates**.

The picture below demonstrates how constraints affect Total Float (Slack) calculations of tasks (without predecessors or successors) against the first task of 10 days duration.

#	Constraint Type	Constraint Date	Total Slack	Late Start	Late Finish
1	As Soon As Possible	NA	0d	Aug 12	Aug 25
2	As Late As Possible	NA	0d	Aug 21	Aug 25
3	Start No Earlier Than	Aug 19	2d	Aug 21	Aug 25
4	Start No Later Than	Aug 19	5d	Aug 19	Aug 21
5	Must Start On	Aug 19	0d	Aug 19	Aug 21
6	Must Finish On	Aug 19	0d	Aug 15	Aug 19
7	Finish No Earlier Than	Aug 20	3d	Aug 21	Aug 25
8	Finish No Later Than	Aug 20	4d	Aug 18	Aug 20
9	As Soon As Possible	NA	2d	Aug 14	Aug 20
10	As Soon As Possible	NA	-2d	Aug 8	Aug 14

Tasks 9 and 10 have a **Deadline Date** assigned which allows a second constraint to be applied to a task and operates like a Finish No Later Than constraint.

The **Late** constraints reduce the amount of Total Float (Slack) a task has and may generate **Negative Float**.

The **Must** constraints act like an Early and Late constraint in one.

10.5 Using Custom Fields

Select the **Project**, **Properties**, **Custom Fields** to open the **Custom Fields** form. This function includes a number of predefined fields for both Task and Resources.

- ❖ Task fields may be used for recording additional information about Tasks (such as responsibility, location, floor, system) and may be displayed in Task Views such as the Gantt Chart.
- ❖ Resource fields may record information such as telephone number, address, office and skills and may be displayed in Resource Views such as the Resource Sheet.
- ❖ The fields may be renamed. For example, the Task Text 1 field may be renamed "Responsibility" and the name of the person responsible for the task (this may not be the resource assigned to the task) placed in the Responsibility (Text 1) column.
- ❖ A renamed field is then available in the Task Information or Resource Information Custom Fields tab.
- ❖ Formulas may be created to populate the task fields with calculated data.
- ❖ Tasks and Resources may be Grouped using Custom Fields.

These predefined fields fall into the following categories: Cost, Date, Duration, Finish (date), Flag, Number, Outline Code, Start (date) and Text.

10.6 Custom Columns Formulas and Drop-Down List

The **Custom Attributes** section of the **Custom Fields** form is used to define Lookup lists and Formulas:

- ❖ The option **None** allows data to be entered, without any restrictions, from either a column or the **Task** or **Resource Information** forms.
- ❖ `Lookup...` opens the **Edit Lookup Table** where a table of values and descriptions may be entered. The Value is displayed in columns and Description in bands when the tasks are grouped by this field. Data entry restrictions may be set here.
- ❖ `Formula...` allows the assigning of formulas for the calculation of field values from other task and project fields.

The **Calculation for task and group summary rows** specifies how Summary Tasks calculate their values, such as Maximum, Minimum, Sum, None and Average:

- ❖ Dates could be Minimum or Maximum, and
- ❖ Cost would use Sum.

Calculation for assignment rows determines if the field value is displayed against the resource or the resource and assignment in Task Usage and Resource Usage fields.

Value to display allows the options of displaying the value in the cell or generating graphical indicators such as traffic lights.

10.7 Creating Graphical Indicators

Graphical Indicators are useful for creating traffic light reports to show, for example, when tasks are ahead or behind the Baseline.

In summary, to create a **Graphical Indicator**:

- ❖ From the **Custom Fields** form rename a **Custom Number Field**,
- ❖ Create a value in this new field using the **Formula** button, such as **Baseline Finish – Finish**,
- ❖ Check the values calculated in a column as you may have to divide the value you obtain by a factor to obtain a sensible answer,
- ❖ Select the **Graphical Indicators** button and use this to set the graphical indicators in columns.

10.8 Custom Outline Codes

There are ten hierarchical Task Custom Outline Codes and ten hierarchical Resource Custom Outline Codes that may be renamed to suit the project requirements.

- ❖ **Task Custom Outline Codes** may be used for any hierarchical project breakdown structure, such as a PRINCE2 Product Breakdown Structure, Contract Breakdown Structure, Work Breakdown Structure and
- ❖ **Resource Custom Outline Codes** may be used for organizational breakdown structures such as the hierarchy of authority, locations and departments.

The process to use this function has the following steps:

- ❖ Define the new Outline Code structure,
- ❖ Assign the codes to the tasks or resources, and
- ❖ Create a Group to organize the tasks under the new Custom Outline Code structure.

10.8.1 Define a Custom Outline Code Structure

Select the **Project**, **Properties**, **Custom Fields**:

- ❖ An Outline Code may be created for either **Task** or **Resource** data by clicking on the appropriate radio button under the title **Field**.
- ❖ Select the Outline Code, the drop-down box in top right-hand side.
- ❖ The `Import Field...` function allows you to copy a code structure from another project in a method similar to Organizer.
- ❖ The `Rename...` button opens a form to edit the name of the Outline Code.
- ❖ The `Lookup...` button opens the **Edit Look Up Table** form for the selected Outline Code to create the **Lookup table**.
- ❖ Define the **Mask** or code structure by clicking on the `Edit Mask...` button at the top right-hand side before entering the codes. This will open the **Outline Code Definition** form where the code structure is defined:
  - ➢ Each **Level** is assigned a number.
  - ➢ The **Sequence** defines the type of text that may be entered for the code: Numbers, Upper Case, Lower Case or Characters (text).
  - ➢ The **Length** specifies how many characters the Code Level may have: any, or a number between 1 and 10.
  - ➢ The **Separator** defines the character that separates each level in the structure.

- ❖ The picture displays 4 levels each using a different option for their code:

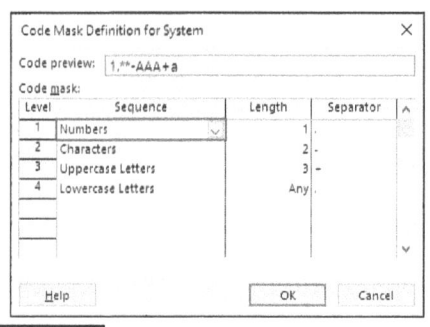

- ❖ Click the **OK** button to return to the **Edit Lookup Table** form where the Code Values and Descriptions are entered. The picture shows two levels for a Power Station Unit and Equipment:

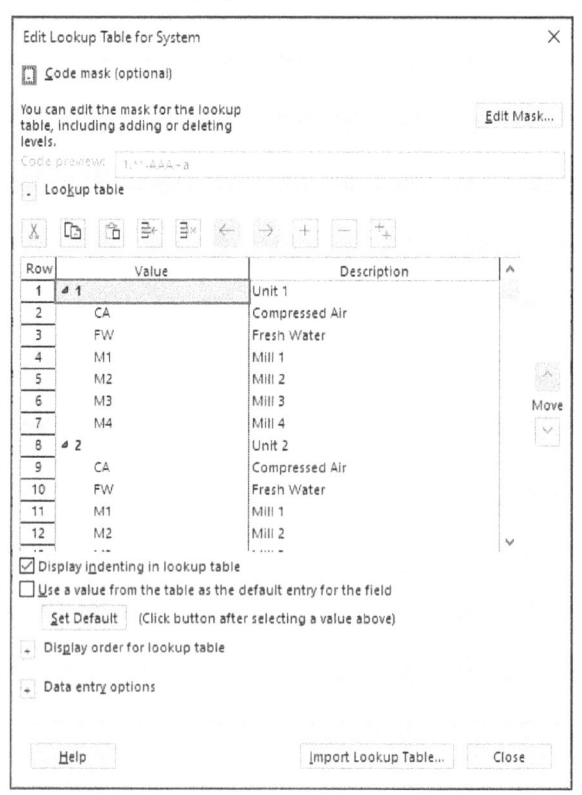

10.8.2 Assigning the Custom Codes

❖ The codes are assigned by:

Displaying the appropriate column:

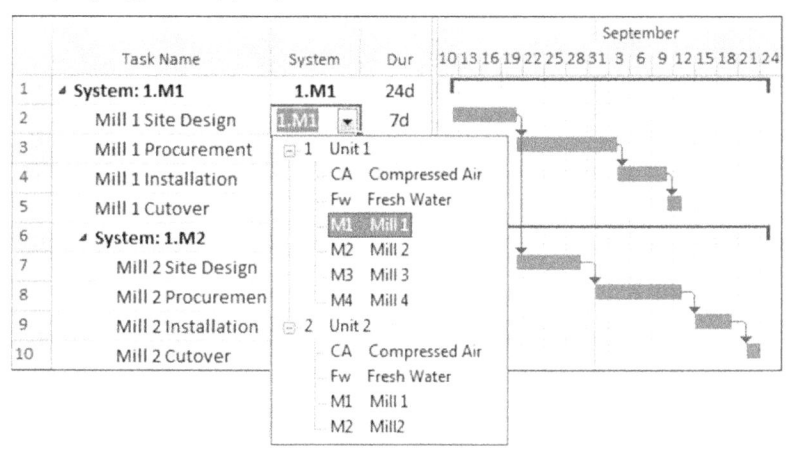

	Task Name	System	Dur
1	▲ System: 1.M1	1.M1	24d
2	Mill 1 Site Design	1.M1	7d
3	Mill 1 Procurement		
4	Mill 1 Installation		
5	Mill 1 Cutover		
6	▲ System: 1.M2		
7	Mill 2 Site Design		
8	Mill 2 Procuremen		
9	Mill 2 Installation		
10	Mill 2 Cutover		

Dropdown:
- 1 Unit 1
  - CA Compressed Air
  - Fw Fresh Water
  - M1 Mill 1
  - M2 Mill 2
  - M3 Mill 3
  - M4 Mill 4
- 2 Unit 2
  - CA Compressed Air
  - Fw Fresh Water
  - M1 Mill 1
  - M2 Mill2

❖ Or by opening the Task Information or Resource Information form:

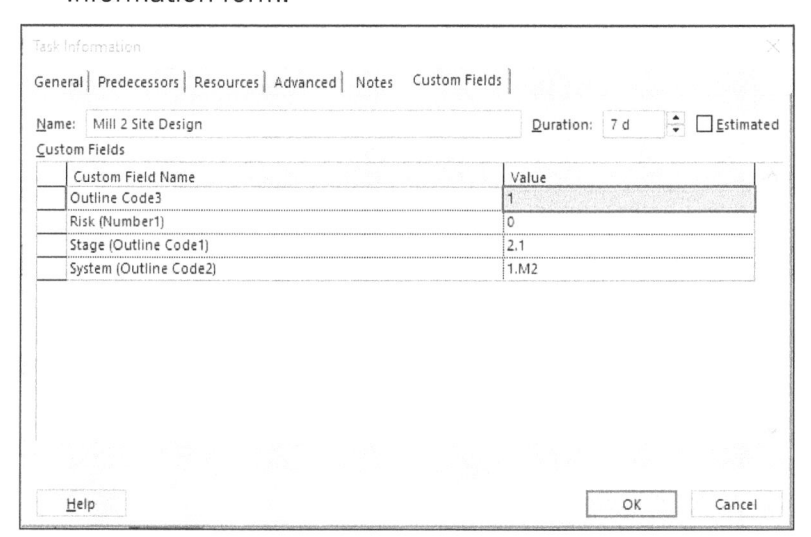

Task Information — Custom Fields tab

Name: Mill 2 Site Design   Duration: 7 d   ☐ Estimated

Custom Field Name	Value
Outline Code3	1
Risk (Number1)	0
Stage (Outline Code1)	2.1
System (Outline Code2)	1.M2

10.8.3 Grouping with Custom Data

Grouping allows grouping of tasks under data items such as Customized fields, Durations, Constraints, etc. This function is useful to group related tasks that are spread throughout a project schedule.

The Grouping function works in a similar way to Filters and Tables. A predefined Group may be assigned by:

- Selecting **View**, **Data**, **Group by:** dropdown to open up a sub menu,
- Then either:
  - Selecting a group from the list, or
  - Selecting **More Groups...** to open the **More Groups** form, clicking on the **Task** or **Resource** radio button, and then selecting one from the list, or

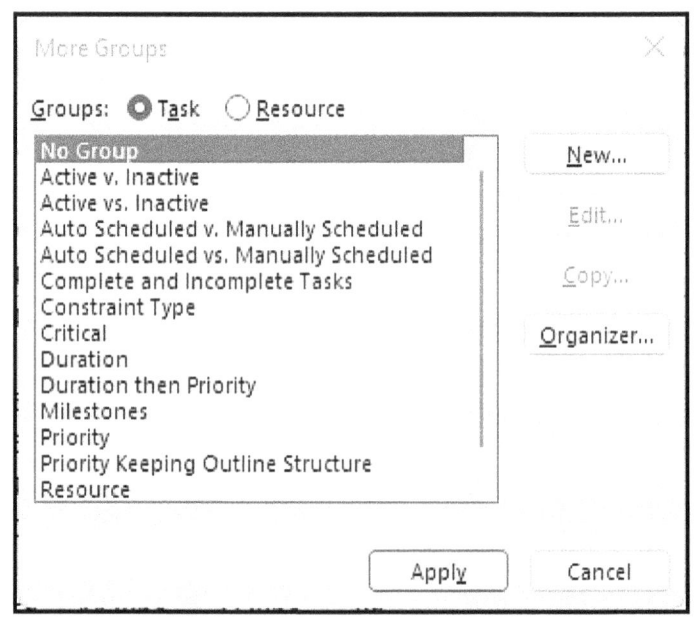

Note: Fields are sorted alphabetically when displayed on the screen, so you may need to be careful with your Code Values and consider prefixing them with a number, so they sort in the order you desire.

To create a new Group:

- ❖ Select **View**, **Data**, **Group by:** dropdown, **New Group By...** to open the **Group Definition** form,
- ❖ Now create a "Grouping" which may be reapplied at a later date or copy to another project using **Organizer**.

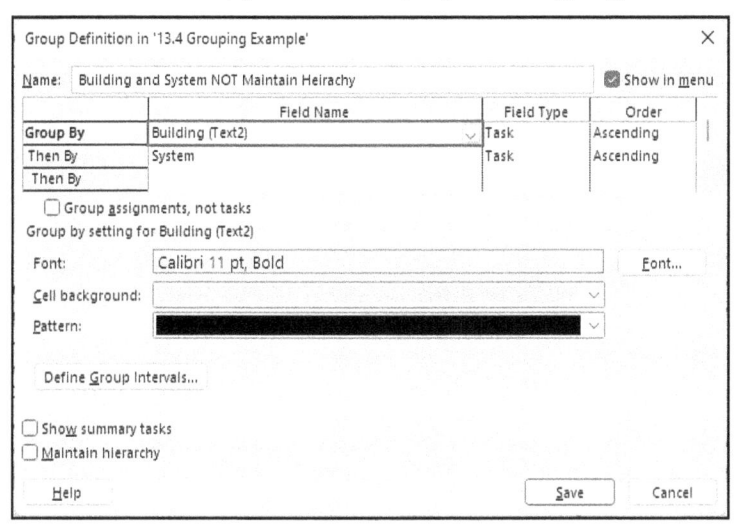

- ❖ The **Define Group Interval** form is available with additional **Group By** options for certain fields, such as Start or Finish. This allows further formatting by defining the intervals of the banding. For example, all the tasks that start in a week or month may be banded together:

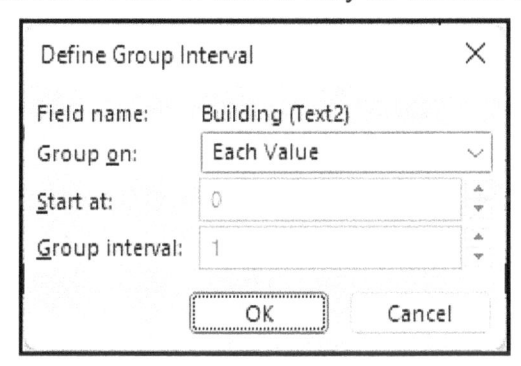

The picture below shows a project Grouped by two text fields that have been renamed Systems and Building. Note the order of the Task IDs:

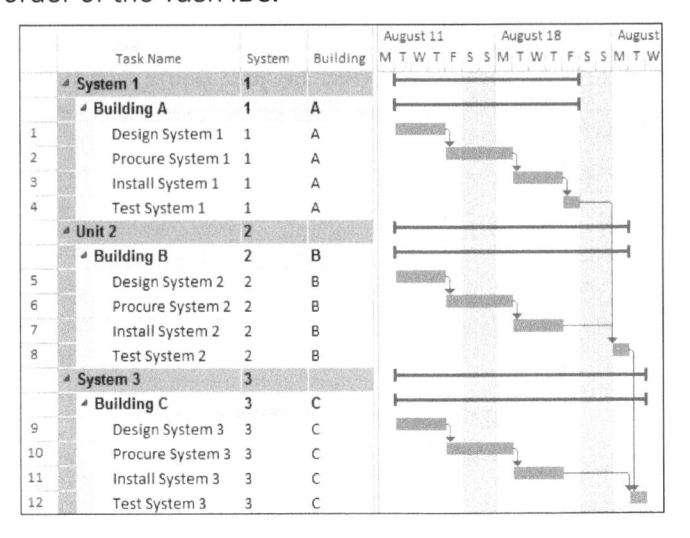

	Task Name	System	Building	August 11 ... August 18 ... August
	▲ System 1	1		
	▲ Building A	1	A	
1	Design System 1	1	A	
2	Procure System 1	1	A	
3	Install System 1	1	A	
4	Test System 1	1	A	
	▲ Unit 2	2		
	▲ Building B	2	B	
5	Design System 2	2	B	
6	Procure System 2	2	B	
7	Install System 2	2	B	
8	Test System 2	2	B	
	▲ System 3	3		
	▲ Building C	3	C	
9	Design System 3	3	C	
10	Procure System 3	3	C	
11	Install System 3	3	C	
12	Test System 3	3	C	

10.8.4 Grouping with Custom Data with AutoFilters

Grouping with one band may also be achieved by turning on the AutoFilter function by either:

- ❖ Selecting **View**, **Data**, **Filter**: and selecting **Display AutoFilter** at the bottom of the list, or
- ❖ Add the **AutoFilter** button to the Quick Assess toolbar and clicking on it.
- ❖ There will now be a down arrow ▼ in the column header,
- ❖ Click on the column header to open the menu,
- ❖ Click on **Group by**,
- ❖ Depending on the data contained in the column you will be offered logical data options to group your tasks,

❖ The picture below displays the options when Grouping by **Duration**:

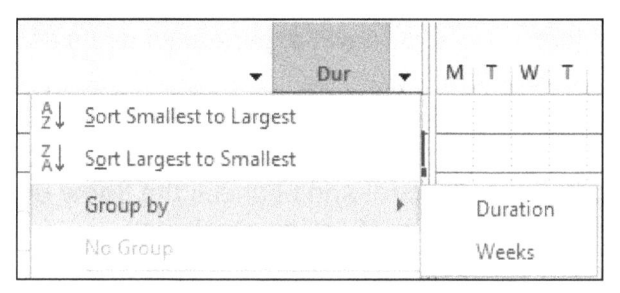

	Dur	M	T	W	T
A↓ Sort Smallest to Largest					
Z↓ Sort Largest to Smallest					
Group by ▶		Duration			
No Group		Weeks			

10.9 Exporting to Excel

The **Analysis** toolbar, designed to export time-phased data to Excel in earlier versions of Microsoft Project, is no longer available in Version 2010 and later.

The options to export to Excel are:

❖ Select the data in Microsoft Project and cut and paste and you have the option of keeping or not keeping the formatting when pasting.

❖ Timescale data may be copied and pasted from the **Resource Usage** and **Task Usage** views, but the date information must be manually added to the Excel Spreadsheet,

❖ The **Report**, **Export**, **Visual Reports** export to Excel in **Pivot Table** format, so you will need to hone up on your Pivot Table skills to use this function.

❖ The **File**, **Save As**, **Excel** format allows the mapping of specific fields to and from an Excel Spreadsheet. **Maps** may be set up and used to map data to and from Microsoft Project and Excel.

10.10 Turning Off Getting Started and other POP ups

These guides often slow down experienced users as they have to be continually closed:

- To prevent the pane titled **Getting Started** from appearing every time Microsoft Project is opened, select **File, Options, General** and uncheck the **Show the start screen when this application starts** box.
- The Help suggestions offered by Microsoft project are often misleading, these should be switched off by selecting **File, Options, Schedule** and unchecking:
- **Show scheduling Messages**,
- **Show task schedule warnings** and
- **Show task schedule suggestions**.
- The select the **Advanced** tab and uncheck **Advice from Planning Wizard**.

10.11 Contingent Time

This topic should be considered, and Contingent Time may be included using a number of techniques:

- Adding one or more tasks that may be reduced in duration to keep the project end date constant as the project progresses and incurs delays.
- Increasing all task durations by a factor.
- Making some calendar work days non-work.

10.12 Earned Value

The method that Microsoft Project uses to calculate the Earned Value data is documented in the Help file and should be read carefully, as different versions of Microsoft calculate these fields differently. Should different Earned Value calculations be required, then Custom Data Fields should be considered as an alternative.

The column calculations should be checked and you will see the way Microsoft Project calculates the values and you may disagree with their method.

	Task Name	SV	CV	EAC	BAC	VAC
1	Bid For Facility Extension	$468.00	-$132.00	$55,979.16	$55,060.00	-$919.16
2	Technical Specification	$468.00	-$132.00	$20,130.53	$19,800.00	-$330.53
3	Approval to Bid	$0.00	$0.00	$0.00	$0.00	$0.00
4	Determine Installat	$0.00	$1,680.00	$5,040.00	$6,720.00	$1,680.00
5	Create Technical Sp	$468.00	-$1,812.00	$21,717.17	$8,600.00	-$13,117.17
6	Identify Supplier Cc	$0.00	$0.00	$1,120.00	$1,120.00	$0.00
7	Validate Technical S	$0.00	$0.00	$3,360.00	$3,360.00	$0.00
8	Delivery Plan	$0.00	$0.00	$21,520.00	$21,520.00	$0.00
14	Bid Document Submit	$0.00	$0.00	$13,740.00	$13,740.00	$0.00

Note: You may wish to use Custom Fields or third party software to calculate these EV fields in a more conventional method.

10.13 Do I Have All the Scope?

Many schedules are unrealistic or do not calculate a realistic Critical Path, because the whole scope has not been entered into a schedule. There are a couple of techniques that may be employed to ensure the whole scope has been included:

- ❖ Stakeholder Analysis, and
- ❖ Risk Analysis.

10.13.1 Stakeholder Analysis

Many project managers conduct a **Stakeholder Analysis** at the start of a project. This process identifies all the people and organizations with an interest in the project and their interests.

- ❖ You may use a stakeholder analysis to identify all the stakeholders and their associated activities. The activities must be included in the schedule.
- ❖ Key project success factors may be identified from the interests of the most influential stakeholders.
- ❖ The stakeholder analysis may be used as the basis of a communications plan.

10.13.2 Risk Analysis

The process of planning a project may identify risks and a formal risk analysis should be considered. A risk analysis may identify risk mitigation activities that should be added to the schedule before it is submitted for approval.

10.14 Preparing for Dispute Resolution

Dispute resolution is becoming more frequent. There are some steps that may be taken to prepare for this eventuality which should reduce the cost of this process.

10.14.1 Keeping Electronic Copies of Each Update

Each time you report to the client or management, it is recommended that you save a copy of your project and change the file name (perhaps by appending a date to the file name or using a revision or version number) or create a subdirectory for each version of the project. This allows you to reproduce these reports at any time in the future and an electronic copy will be available for dispute resolution purposes.

10.14.2 Clearly Record the Effect of Each Change

Each change should be clearly recorded. Consider if you should:

- Create a copy of the schedule for each scope change analysis,
- Set the Baseline before entering scope changes,
- For clarity add new task/s for the scope changes and do not extend existing tasks,
- Show delays as tasks, not as lags or constraints,
- Ensure when the elapsed duration of the delay is required calculate this by placing a delay Milestone on a 7day per week calendar.

11 INDEX

% Complete 88
% Lags 45
% Work 88
Actual costs are always calculated by Microsoft Project? 104, 105
Add Progress Line 94
Add space before label 63, 73
Add to Quick Access Toolbar 12
Always roll up Gantt bars 54
As Late As Possible Constraint ... 33
Auto Schedule button 10
Auto Scheduled 10
AutoFilters 36
Autolink inserted or moved tasks 6, 9
Bar Formatting 53
Bars
    Baseline 97, 98
    Format Style 31
    Height 53
    Negative Float 32
    Styles 76
    Text 56
Baseline 85
Calculate multiple critical paths . 61
Calculated Filters 34
Calendar Non Work Days 5
Calendar Task 18
Change Working Time 15, 20
Change Working Time form 22
Collapse the Ribbon 11, 110
Colors Format 58
Concatenate 25
Contingent Time 124
Current Date 8, 90
Custom Fields 57
Custom Outline Codes 116
Customize Fields Form 114
Customize Quick Access Toolbar 11
Customize the Ribbon..., ... 110
Data Date 86
Date
    Format 50, 53
    On Bars 53
Deadline Date 30
Default end time: 22
Default start time: 22
Default task type: 80
Define Group Interval form 121
Delete Key 1
Dispute Resolution 127
Driving Predecessors 47
Driving Relationships 46

Driving Successors, ... 47
Duration is entered in: 17
Dynamically Linking Cells 111
Earned Value 90, 125
Effort driven 81
Elapsed Durations 42
Elapsed Leads and Lags 43
Excel 123
Exporting 123
Featured Templates 108
Filter Calculated 34
Finish Milestone 38
Finish No Earlier Than constraint .. 1
Finish Variance 23, 69
Fixed
    Duration Task Type 79
    Units Task Type 79
    Work Task Type 79
Fixed Costs 105
Float 19
Float Bars 32
Form
    Customize Fields 114
    Define Group Interval 121
    Format Bar 31
    More Groups 120
    Project Statistics 94
    Timescale 68
Format
    Bar Style 31
    Baseline Bar 97, 98, 100
    Date 50
    Nonworking Time 68
Free Float 31
Gantt Chart Wizard 5, 33, 97, 98
Global.mpt 9, 106, 109
Graphical Indicator 116
Gridlines Colors 58
Hammock 41
Hide rollup bars when summary expanded 54
Hide task bar 65
Hiding Text 65
Hours per day: 16, 17
Hyperlink Colors 58
Import/Export 12, 76
Inactive 65
Indent Name 62, 63
Indicators column 2, 18
Interactive Filters 36
Interim Plan 85
Ladder scheduling 44
Lags 19
Legacy Format 5
Legend 76

129   © *Eastwood Harris*

LEO Task 41	Show Quick Access Toolbar
Level Of Effort 41	Below the Ribbon 11
LTR.. 60	Show scheduling Messages 124
Macros 109	Show task schedule suggestions 124
Manual Page Breaks.................... 76	Show task schedule warnings .. 124
Manually Scheduled.................... 10	Split
Maps..................................... 109, 123	Removing a Bar Split.................. 28
Mark as a milestone 39	Show Bar Splits........................... 29
Mark as a Milestone 40	Task 27
Mark on Track...................... 99, 101	Split in-progress tasks....
Milestones 38	.... 3, 9, 27, 92, 93, 95
Minimize the Ribbon 11	Stakeholder Analysis................. 126
Modules 109	Start Milestone 38
Move start of remaining parts before status date forward to status date 96	Start No Earlier Than constraint... 1
	Start on Current Date 8
	Start on Project Start Date............ 8
mpt File Type 107	Status Date 8, 86, 90
Multiple Critical Paths................. 61	Task Calendar 18
Negative Float.............................. 31	Task Drivers 46
New tasks created: 10	Task Information.......................... 18
Non Effort driven 81	Task Inspector 46, 47
Non-driving Relationships........... 46	Task Mode 10
Nonworking Time......................... 68	Task Path.......................... 46, 47, 49
Nonworking Time Colors............. 58	Task Splitting 25
Organizer Overview 109	Task Type
Page Breaks................................. 76	Fixed Duration............................ 79
Paste Link 111	Fixed Units.................................. 79
Personal Template 107, 108	Fixed Work.................................. 79
Personal Templates 108	Task Usage View........................ 105
Physical % Complete 89	Tasks will always honor their constraint dates........ 3, 4, 9, 95
Predecessor Unique ID 64	
Progress Lines 94, 97	Templates.................................... 107
Project Information form............. 14	Text Colors................................... 58
Project Start Date 8	Text Wrapping 59
Project Statistics......................... 94	Timescale 68
Project, Project Information form 21	Timescale Format Colors 58
Quick Access Toolbar 11, 110	Touch/Mouse Mode 13
Relationship Diagram 46, 48	Tracing the Logic.......................... 48
Relationships Driving.................. 46	Tracking Toolbar 93
Remaining Duration 87	Unique ID....................................... 64
Reports.. 123	Predecessor 64
Reschedule uncompleted tasks to start after:....................... 104	Successor.................................... 64
	Units... 63
Reschedule uncompleted work to start after:......................... 92	Units per Time Period............ 79, 80
	Update as Scheduled .. 93, 99, 101
Reschedule Work 93, 101	Update Project form 91, 98
Resource Usage View................ 105	Update Tasks 94
Retained Logic............................. 27	Updating task status updates resource status............ 95, 103
Risk Analysis.............................. 126	
Roll up Gantt bar to summary 55	Variance Duration........................ 85
Round Bars to Whole Days......... 55	Variance Finish 85
RTL... 60	Variance Start,............................. 85
Schedule Options 9	Visual Basic Macros 109
Scheduling ignores resource calendars 15, 18, 20, 21	Visual Reports............................ 123
	Wildcard 35
S-Curve 71	Wrap Text 59
Show project summary task 72	Zoom Slider 67

130   © *Eastwood Harris*

Lightning Source UK Ltd.
Milton Keynes UK
UKHW020651050722
405403UK00010B/832